ARCHITECT REGISTRATION EXAM

BUILDING DESIGN & CONSTRUCTION SYSTEMS

ARE SAMPLE PROBLEMS AND PRACTICE EXAM

SECOND EDITION

DAVID KENT BALLAST, FAIA
HOLLY WILLIAMS LEPPO, RA/CID

The Power to Pass®
www.ppi2pass.com

Professional Publications, Inc. • Belmont, California

Benefit by Registering This Book with PPI

- Get book updates and corrections.
- Hear the latest exam news.
- Obtain exclusive exam tips and strategies.
- Receive special discounts.

Register your book at **www.ppi2pass.com/register**.

Report Errors and View Corrections for This Book

PPI is grateful to every reader who notifies us of a possible error. Your feedback allows us to improve the quality and accuracy of our products. You can report errata and view corrections at **www.ppi2pass.com/errata**.

BUILDING DESIGN & CONSTRUCTION SYSTEMS: ARE SAMPLE PROBLEMS AND PRACTICE EXAM Second Edition

Current printing of this edition: 2

Printing History

edition number	printing number	update
1	4	Minor corrections. Copyright update.
2	1	New edition. Code update. Copyright update.
2	2	Minor corrections.

PPI
1250 Fifth Avenue, Belmont, CA 94002
(650) 593-9119
www.ppi2pass.com

ISBN: 978-1-59126-325-8

Library of Congress Control Number: 2010941101

TABLE OF CONTENTS

PREFACE AND ACKNOWLEDGMENTS

This book is tailored to the needs of those studying for the Architect Registration Examination (ARE). For the second edition, we have updated the content to reflect the July 2011 update of the *ARE 4.0 Guidelines*, as well as the most recent editions of a number of codes and standards, including

- 2005 *Americans with Disabilities Act and Architectural Barriers Act Accessibility Guidelines*
- 2008 ACI 318 *Building Code Requirements for Structural Concrete*
- 2009 *International Building Code*
- 2010 CSI MasterFormat

In the ARE, there is considerable overlap in what you need to study for the various divisions. For this reason, the *ARE Review Manual* covers all the divisions of the ARE in a single volume. This book, *Building Design & Construction Systems: ARE Sample Problems and Practice Exam*, is one of seven companion volumes, one for each ARE division. We believe that this organization will help you study for individual divisions most effectively.

You will find that this book and the related volumes are valuable parts of your exam preparation. Although there is no substitute for a good formal education and the broad-based experience provided by your internship with a practicing architect, this review series will help you direct your study efforts to increase your chances of passing the ARE.

Many people have helped in the production of this book. We would like to thank all the fine people at PPI including Scott Marley (project editor), Cathy Schrott (typesetter), Amy Schwertman (cover designer and illustrator), and Thomas Bergstrom (illustrator).

Although we had much help in preparing this new edition, the responsibility for any errors is our own. A current list of known errata for this book is maintained at **www.ppi2pass.com/errata**, and you can let us know of any errors you find at the same place. We greatly appreciate the time our readers take to help us keep this book accurate and up to date.

David Kent Ballast, FAIA
Holly Williams Leppo, RA/CID

INTRODUCTION

ABOUT THIS BOOK

Building Design & Construction Systems: ARE Sample Problems and Practice Exam is written to help you prepare for the Building Design & Construction Systems division of the Architect Registration Examination (ARE).

Although this book can be a valuable study aid by itself, it is designed to be used along with the *ARE Review Manual*, also published by PPI. The *ARE Review Manual* is organized into sections that cover all seven divisions of the ARE.

- Programming, Planning & Practice
- Site Planning & Design
- Schematic Design
- Structural Systems
- Building Systems
- Building Design & Construction Systems
- Construction Documents & Services

This book is one of seven companion volumes to the *ARE Review Manual* that PPI publishes. Each of these books contains sample problems and practice exams for one of the ARE divisions.

- *Programming, Planning & Practice: ARE Sample Problems and Practice Exam*
- *Site Planning & Design: ARE Sample Problems and Practice Exam*
- *Schematic Design: ARE Sample Problems and Practice Exam*
- *Structural Systems: ARE Sample Problems and Practice Exam*
- *Building Systems: ARE Sample Problems and Practice Exam*
- *Building Design & Construction Systems: ARE Sample Problems and Practice Exam*
- *Construction Documents & Services: ARE Sample Problems and Practice Exam*

THE ARCHITECT REGISTRATION EXAMINATION

Congratulations on completing (or nearing the end of) the Intern Development Program! You are two-thirds of the way to being able to call yourself an architect. NAAB degree? Check. IDP? Check. Now on to step three.

The final hurdle is the Architect Registration Examination. The ARE is a uniform test administered to candidates who wish to become licensed architects after they have served their required internships. It is given throughout the United States, the U.S. territories, and Canada.

The ARE has been developed to protect the health, safety, and welfare of the public by testing a candidate's entry-level competence to practice architecture. Its content relates as closely as possible to situations encountered in practice. It tests for the kinds of knowledge, skills, and abilities required of an entry-level architect, with particular emphasis on those services that affect public health, safety, and welfare. In order to accomplish these objectives, the exam tests for

- knowledge in specific subject areas
- the ability to make decisions
- the ability to consolidate and use information to solve a problem
- the ability to coordinate the activities of others on the building team

The ARE also includes some professional practice and project management problems, and problems that are based on particular editions of codes as specified in the *ARE 4.0 Guidelines*. (However, the editions specified by the *ARE Guidelines* are not necessarily the most current editions available.)

The ARE is developed jointly by the National Council of Architectural Registration Boards (NCARB) and the Committee of Canadian Architectural Councils (CCAC), with the assistance of Prometric. Prometric serves as NCARB's test development and operations consultant and operates and maintains the test centers where the ARE is administered.

Although the responsibility of professional licensing rests with each individual state, every state's board requires successful completion of the ARE to achieve registration or licensure. One of the primary reasons for a uniform test is to facilitate reciprocity—that is, to enable an architect to more easily gain a license to practice in states other than the one in which he or she was originally licensed.

The ARE is administered and graded entirely by computer. All divisions of the exam are offered six days a week at a network of test centers across North America. The results are scored by computer, and the results are forwarded to individual state boards of architecture, which process them and send them to candidates. If you fail a division, you must wait six months before you can retake that division.

First Steps

As you begin to prepare for the exam, you should first obtain a current copy of the *ARE Guidelines* from NCARB. This booklet will get you started with the exam process and will be a valuable reference throughout. It includes descriptions of the seven divisions, instructions on how to apply, pay for, and take the ARE, and other useful information. You can download a PDF version at www.ncarb.org, or you can request a printed copy through the contact information provided at that site.

The NCARB website also gives current information about the exam, education requirements, training, examination procedures, and NCARB reciprocity services. It includes sample scenarios of the computer-based examination process and examples of costs associated with taking the computer-based exam.

The PPI website is also a good source of answers to frequently asked questions about the exam (at **www.ppi2pass.com/arefaq**).

To register as an examinee, you should obtain the registration requirements from the board in the state, province, or territory where you want to be registered. The exact requirements vary from one jurisdiction to another, so contact your local board. Links to state boards can be found at **www.ppi2pass.com/faqs/architecture-state-boards**.

As soon as NCARB has verified your qualifications and you have received your "Authorization to Test" letter, you may begin scheduling examinations. The exams are offered on a first come, first served basis and must be scheduled at least 72 hours in advance. See the *ARE Guidelines* for instructions on finding a current list of testing centers. You may take the exams at any location, even outside the state in which you intend to become registered.

You may schedule any division of the ARE at any time and may take the divisions in any order. Divisions can be taken one at a time, to spread out preparation time and exam costs, or can be taken together in any combination.

However, you must pass all seven divisions of the ARE within a single five-year period. This period, or "rolling clock," begins on the date of the first division you passed. If you have not completed the ARE within five years, the divisions that you passed more than five years ago are no longer credited, and the content in them must be retaken. Your new five-year period begins on the date of the earliest division you passed within the last five years.

Examination Format

The ARE is organized into seven divisions that test various areas of architectural knowledge and problem-solving ability.

Programming, Planning & Practice

    85 multiple-choice problems
    1 graphic vignette: Site Zoning

Site Planning & Design

    65 multiple-choice problems
    2 graphic vignettes: Site Design, Site Grading

Schematic Design

    2 graphic vignettes: Building Layout, Interior Layout

Structural Systems

    125 multiple-choice problems
    1 graphic vignette: Structural Layout

Building Systems

    95 multiple-choice problems
    1 graphic vignette: Mechanical & Electrical Plan

Building Design & Construction Systems

    85 multiple-choice problems
    3 graphic vignettes: Accessibility/Ramp, Roof Plan, Stair Design

Construction Documents & Services

    100 multiple-choice problems
    1 graphic vignette: Building Section

Experienced test-takers will tell you that there is quite a bit of overlap among these divisions. Problems that seem better suited to the Construction Documents & Services division may show up on the Building Design & Construction Systems division, for example, and problems on architectural history and building regulations might show up anywhere. That's why it's important to have a comprehensive strategy for studying and taking the exams.

The ARE is given entirely by computer. There are two kinds of problems on the exam. Multiple-choice problems are short questions presented on the computer screen; you answer them by clicking on the right answer or answers, or by filling in a blank. Graphic vignettes are longer problems in design; you solve a vignette by planning and drawing your solution on the computer. Six of the seven divisions contain both multiple-choice sections and graphic vignettes; the Schematic Design division contains only vignettes. Both kinds of problems are described later in this Introduction.

STUDY GUIDELINES

After the five to seven years (or even more) of higher education you've received to this point, you probably have a good idea of the study strategy that works best for you. The trick is figuring out how to apply that to the ARE. Unlike many college courses, there isn't a textbook or set of class notes from which all the exam problems will be derived. The exams are very broad and draw problems from multiple areas of knowledge.

The first challenge, then, is figuring out what to study. The ARE is never quite the same exam twice. The field of knowledge tested is always the same, but the specific problems asked are drawn randomly from a large pool, and will differ from one candidate to the next. One division may contain many code-related problems for one candidate and only a few for the next. This makes the ARE a challenge to study for.

The *ARE Guidelines* contain lists of resources recommended by NCARB. That list can seem overwhelming, though, and on top of that, many of the recommended books are expensive or no longer in print. To help address this problem, PPI has published the *ARE Review Manual*, which gives you an overview of the concepts and information that will be most useful in preparing for the ARE. A list of helpful resources for preparing for the Building Design & Construction Systems division can also be found in the Recommended Reading section of this book.

Your method of studying for the ARE should be based on both the content and form of the exam and on your school and work experience. Because the exam covers such a broad range of subject matter, it cannot possibly include every detail of practice. Rather, it tends to focus on what is considered entry-level knowledge and knowledge that is important for the protection of the public's health, safety, and welfare. Other types of problems are asked, too, but this knowledge should be the focus of your review schedule.

Your recent work experience should also help you determine what areas to study the most. If, for example, you have been working with construction documents for several years, you will probably need less review in that area than in others you have not had much recent experience with.

The *ARE Review Manual* and its companion volumes are structured to help you focus on the topics that are more likely to be included in the exam in one form or another. Some subjects may seem familiar or may be easy to recall from memory, and others may seem completely foreign; the latter are the ones to give particular attention to. It may be wise to study additional sources on these subjects, take review seminars, or get special help from someone who is knowledgeable in the topic.

A typical candidate might spend about forty hours preparing for and taking each exam. Some will need to study more, some less. Forty hours is about one week of studying eight hours a day, or two weeks of four hours a day, or a month of two hours a day, along with reasonable breaks and time to attend to other responsibilities. As you probably work full time and have other family and personal obligations, it is important to develop a realistic schedule and do your best to stick to it. The ARE is not the kind of exam you can cram for the night before.

Also, since the fees are high and retaking a test is expensive, you want to do your best and pass in as few tries as possible. Allowing enough time to study and going into each exam well prepared will help you relax and concentrate on the problems.

The following steps may provide a useful structure for an exam study program.

Step 1: Start early. You can't review for a test like this by starting two weeks before the date. This is especially true if you are taking all portions of the exam for the first time.

Step 2: Go through the *ARE Review Manual* quickly to get a feeling for the scope of the subject matter and how the major topics are organized. Whatever division you're studying for, plan to review the chapters on building regulations as well. Review the *ARE Guidelines*.

Step 3: Based on your review of the *ARE Review Manual* and *ARE Guidelines*, and on a realistic appraisal of your strong and weak areas, set priorities for study and determine which topics need more study time.

Step 4: Divide review subjects into manageable units and organize them into a sequence of study. It is generally best to start with the less familiar subjects. Based on the exam date and plans for beginning study, assign a time limit to each study unit. Again, your knowledge of a subject should determine the time devoted to it. You may want to devote an entire week to earthquake design if it is an unfamiliar subject, and only one day to timber design if it is a familiar one. In setting up a schedule, be realistic about other life commitments as well as your personal ability to concentrate on studying over a length of time.

Step 5: Begin studying, and stick with the schedule. Of course, this is the most difficult part of the process and the one that requires the most self-discipline. The job should be easier if you have started early and if you are following a realistic schedule that allows time for recreation and personal commitments.

Step 6: Stop studying a day or two before the exam. Relax. By this time, no amount of additional cramming will help.

At some point in your studying, you will want to spend some time becoming familiar with the program you will be using to solve the graphic vignettes, which does not resemble commercial CAD software. The software and sample vignettes can be downloaded from the NCARB website at www.ncarb.org.

There are many schools of thought on the best order for taking the divisions. One factor to consider is the six-month waiting period before you can retake a particular division. It's never fun to predict what you might fail, but if you know that a specific area might give you trouble, consider taking that exam near the beginning. You might be pleasantly surprised when you check the mailbox, but if not, as you work through the rest of the exams, the clock will be ticking and you can schedule the retest six months later.

Here are some additional tips.

- Learn concepts first, and then details later. For example, it is much better to understand the basic ideas and theories of waterproofing than it is to attempt to memorize dozens of waterproofing products and details. Once the concept is clear, the details are much easier to learn and to apply during the exam.

- Use the *ARE Review Manual's* index to focus on particular subjects in which you feel weak, especially subjects that can apply to more than one division.

- Don't tackle all your hardest subjects first. Make one of your early exams one that you feel fairly confident about. It's nice to get off on the right foot with a PASS.

- Programming, Planning & Practice and Building Design & Construction Systems both tend to be "catch-all" divisions that cover a lot of material from the Construction Documents & Services division as well as others. Consider taking Construction Documents & Services first among those three, and then the other two soon after.

- Many past candidates recommend taking the Programming, Planning & Practice division last or nearly last, so that you will be familiar with the body of knowledge for all the other divisions as well.

- Brush up on architectural history before taking any of the divisions with multiple-choice sections. Know major buildings and their architects, particularly structures that are representative of an architect's philosophy (for example, Le Corbusier and the Villa Savoye) or that represent "firsts" or "turning points."

- Try to schedule your exams so that you'll have enough time to get yourself ready, eat, and review a little. If you'll have a long drive to the testing center, try to avoid having to make it during rush hour.

- If you are planning to take more than one division at a time, do not overstudy any one portion of the exam. It is generally better to review the concepts than to try to become an overnight expert in one area. For example, you may need to know general facts about plate girders, but you will not need to know how to complete a detailed design of a plate girder.

- Even though you may have a good grasp of the information and knowledge in a particular subject area, be prepared to address problems on the material in a variety of forms and from different points of view. For example, you may have studied and know definitions, but you will also need to be able to apply that knowledge when a problem includes a definition-type word as part of a more complex situation-type of problem.

- Solve as many sample problems as possible, including those provided with NCARB's practice program, the books of sample problems and practice exams published by PPI, and any others that are available.

- Take advantage of the community of intern architects going through this experience with you. Some local AIA chapters offer ARE preparation courses or may be able to help you organize a study group with other interns in your area. PPI's Passing Zones are interactive online reviews to help you prepare for individual divisions of the ARE. Find out more at **www.ppi2pass.com/passingzone**.

Visit website forums to discuss the exam with others who have taken it or are preparing to take it. The Architecture Exam Forum at **www.ppi2pass.com/areforum** is a great online resource for questions, study advice, and encouragement. Even though the special problems on the ARE change daily, it is a good idea to get a feeling for the ARE's format, its general emphasis, and the subject areas that previous candidates have found particularly troublesome.

- A day or two before the first test session, stop studying in order to relax as much as possible. Get plenty of sleep the night before the test.

- Try to relax as much as possible during study periods and during the exam itself. Worrying is counterproductive. Candidates who have worked diligently in school, have obtained a wide range of experience during internship, and have started exam review early will be in the best possible position to pass the ARE.

TAKING THE EXAM

What to Bring

Bring multiple forms of photo ID and your Authorization to Test letter to the test site.

It is neither necessary nor permitted to bring any reference materials or scratch paper into the test site. Pencils and scratch paper are provided by the proctor and must be returned when leaving the exam room. Earplugs will also be provided. Leave all your books and notes in the car. Most testing centers have lockers for your keys, small personal belongings, and cell phone.

Do not bring a calculator into the test site. A calculator built into the testing software will be available in all divisions.

Arriving at the Testing Center

Allow plenty of time to get to the exam site, to avoid transportation problems such as getting lost or stuck in traffic jams. If you can, arrive a little early, and take a little time in the parking lot to review one last time the formulas and other things you need to memorize. Then relax, take a few deep breaths, and go take the exam.

Once at the test site, you will check in with the attendant, who will verify your identification and your Authorization to Test. (Don't forget to take this home with you after each exam; you'll need it for the next one.) After you check in, you'll be shown to your testing station.

When the exam begins, you will have the opportunity to click through a tutorial that explains how the computer program works. You'll probably want to read through it the first time, but after that initial exam, you will know how the software works and you won't need the tutorial. Take a deep breath, organize your paper and pencils, and take advantage of the opportunity to dump all the facts floating around in your brain onto your scratch paper—write down as much as you can.

This includes formulas, ratios ("if x increases, y decreases"), and so on—anything that you are trying desperately not to forget. If you can get all the things you've crammed at the last minute onto that paper, you'll be able to think a little more clearly about the problems posed on the screen.

Taking the Multiple-Choice Sections

The ARE multiple-choice sections include several types of problems.

One type of multiple-choice problem is based on written, graphic, or photographic information. You will need to examine the information and select the correct answer from four given options. Some problems may require calculations.

A second type of multiple-choice problem lists four or five items or statements, which are given Roman numerals from I to IV or I to V. For example, the problem may give five statements about a subject, and you must choose the statements that are true. The four answer choices are combinations of these numerals, such as "I and III" or "II, IV, and V."

A third type of multiple-choice problem describes a situation that could be encountered in actual practice. Drawings, diagrams, photographs, forms, tables, or other data may also be given. The problem requires you to select the best answer from four options.

Two kinds of problems that NCARB calls "alternate item types" also show up in the multiple-choice sections. In a "fill in the blank" problem, you must fill a blank with a number derived from a table or calculation. In a "check all that apply" problem, six options are given, and you must choose all the correct answers. The problem tells how many of the options are correct, from two to four. You must choose all the correct answers to receive credit; partial credit is not given.

Between 10% and 15% of the problems in a multiple-choice section will be these "alternate item type" problems. Every problem on the ARE, however, counts the same toward your total score.

Keep in mind that multiple-choice problems often require the examinee to do more than just select an answer based on memory. At times it will be necessary to combine several facts, analyze data, perform a calculation, or review a drawing. You will probably not need the entire time allotted for the multiple-choice sections. If you have time for more than one pass through the problems, you can make good use of it.

Here are some tips for the multiple-choice problems.

- Go through the entire section in one somewhat swift pass, answering the problems that you're sure about and marking the others so you can return to them later. If a problem requires calculations, skip it for now unless it's very simple. Then go back to the beginning and work your way through the exam again, taking a little more time to read each problem and think through the answer.

- Another benefit of going through the entire section at the beginning is that occasionally there is information in one problem that may help you answer another problem somewhere else.

- If you are very unsure of a problem, pick your best answer, mark it, and move on. You will probably have time at the end of the test to go back and recheck these answers. But remember, your first response is usually the best.

- Always answer all the problems. Unanswered problems are counted wrong, so even if you are just guessing, it's better to choose an answer and have a chance of it being correct than to skip it and be certain of getting it wrong. When faced with four options, the old SAT strategy of eliminating the two options that are definitely wrong and making your best guess between the two that remain is helpful on the ARE, too.

- Some problems may seem too simple. Although a few very easy and obvious problems are included on the ARE, more often the simplicity should serve as a red flag to warn you to reevaluate the problem for exceptions to a rule or special circumstances that make the obvious, easy response incorrect.

- Watch out for absolute words in a problem, such as "always," "never," and "completely." These are often a clue that some little exception exists, turning what reads like a true statement into a false one or vice versa.

- Be alert for words like "seldom," "usually," "best," and "most reasonable." These indicate that some judgment will be involved in answering the problem. Look for two or more options that appear to be very similar.

- Some divisions will provide an on-screen reference sheet with useful formulas and other information that will help you solve some problems. Skim through the reference sheet so you know what information is there, and then use it as a resource.

- Occasionally there may be a defective problem. This does not happen very often, but if it does, make the best choice possible under the circumstances. Flawed problems are usually discovered, and either they are not counted on the test or any one of the correct answers is credited.

Solving the Vignettes

Each of the eleven graphic vignettes on the ARE is designed to test a particular area of knowledge and skill. Each one presents a base plan of some kind and gives programmatic and other requirements. You must create a plan that satisfies the requirements. There are three Building Design & Construction Systems vignettes.

The *Accessibility/Ramp vignette* tests your understanding of accessibility requirements as they relate to the design of ramp and stair systems. The problem presents a base plan, a program, and code requirements, and you must design a stair and ramp system connecting two floor elevations.

In the *Roof Plan vignette*, you must demonstrate understanding of the basic concepts related to roof design by completing the roof plan for a small building. You are given the outline of the roof, a background floor plan, and a program, and must complete the roof plan by indicating slopes, directions and elevations, and the locations of roof accessories and equipment.

The *Stair Design vignette* tests your understanding of the three-dimensional nature of stair design and of the basic functional and code issues involved. The problem presents partial background floor plans of two levels, a building section, a program, and code requirements. You must complete the floor plan with a stair system.

The computer scores the vignettes by a complex grading method. Design criteria are given various point values, and responses are categorized as Acceptable, Unacceptable, or Indeterminate.

General Tips for the Vignettes

Here are some general tips for approaching the vignettes. More detailed solving tips can be found in the vignette solutions in this book.

- Remember that with the current format and computer grading, each vignette covers only a very specific area of knowledge and offers a limited number of possible solutions. In a few cases only one solution is really possible. Use this as an advantage.

- Read everything thoroughly, twice. Follow the requirements exactly, letting each problem solve itself as much as possible. Be careful not to read more into the instructions than is there. The test writers are very specific about what they want; there is no need to add to the vignette requirements. If a particular type of solution is strongly suggested, follow that lead.

- Consider only those code requirements given in the vignette, even if they deviate from familiar codes. Do not read anything more into the vignette. The code requirements may be slightly different from what you use in practice.

- Use the scratch paper provided to sketch possible solutions before starting the final solution.

- Make sure all programmed elements are included in the final design.

- When the functional requirements of the vignette have been solved, use the vignette directions as a checklist to make sure all criteria have been satisfied.

General Tips for Using the Vignette Software

It is important to practice with the vignette software that will be used in the exam. The program is unique to the ARE and unlike standard CAD software. If you are unfamiliar with the software interface you will waste valuable time learning to use it, and are likely to run out of time before completing the vignettes. Practice software can be downloaded at no charge from NCARB's website at www.ncarb.org. Usage time for the practice program can also be purchased at Prometric test centers. The practice software includes tutorials, directions, and one practice vignette for each of the eleven vignettes.

Here are some general tips for using the vignette software.

- When elements overlap on the screen, it may be difficult to select a particular element. If this happens, repeatedly click on the element without moving the mouse until the desired element is highlighted.

- Try to stay in "ortho" mode. This mode can be used to solve most vignettes, and it makes the solution process much easier and quicker. Unless obviously required by the vignette, creating additional angles only complicates things and eats up your limited time.

- If the vignette relates to contour modifications, it may help to draw schematic sections through the significant existing slopes. This provides a three-dimensional image of the situation.

- When drawing, if the program states that elements should connect, make sure they touch at their boundaries only and do not overlap. Use the *check* tool to determine if there are any overlaps. Walls that do not align correctly can cause a solution to be downgraded or even rejected. Remember, walls between spaces change color temporarily when properly aligned.

- Make liberal use of the *zoom* tool for sizing and aligning components accurately. Zoom in as closely

as possible on the area being worked. When aligning objects, it is also helpful to use the full-screen cursor.

- Turn on the grid and verify spacing. This makes it easier to align objects and get a sense of the sizes of objects and the distances between them. Use the *measure* tool to check exact measurements if needed.

- Make liberal use of the sketch tools. These can be turned on and off and do not count during the grading, but they can be used to show relationships and for temporary guidelines and other notations.

- Use sketch circles to show required distances, setbacks, clearances, and similar measures.

AFTER THE EXAM

When you've clicked the button to end the test, the computer may prompt you to provide some demographic information about yourself and your education and experience. Then gather your belongings, turn in your scratch paper and materials—you must leave them with the proctor—and leave the test site. (For security reasons, you can't remove anything from the test site.) If the staff has retained your Authorization to Test and your identification, don't forget to retrieve both.

If you should encounter any problems during the exam or have any concerns, be sure to report them to the test site administrator and to NCARB as soon as possible. If you wait longer than ten days after you test, NCARB will not respond to your complaint. You must report your complaint immediately and directly to NCARB and copy your state registration board for any hope of assistance.

Then it's all over but the wait for the mail. How long it takes to get your scores will vary with the efficiency of your state registration board, which reviews the scores from NCARB before passing along the results. But four to six weeks is typical.

As you may have heard from classmates and colleagues, the ARE is a difficult exam—but it is certainly not impossible to pass. A solid architectural education and a well-rounded internship are the best preparation you can have. Watch carefully and listen to the vocabulary used by architects with more experience. Look for opportunities to participate in all phases of project delivery so that you have some "real world" experience to apply to the scenarios you will inevitably find on the exam.

One last piece of advice is not to put off taking the exams. Take them as soon as you become eligible. You will probably still remember a little bit from your college courses and you may even have your old textbooks and notes handy. As life gets more complicated—with spouses and children and work obligations—it is easy to make excuses and never find time to get around to it. Make the commitment, and do it now. After all, this is the last step to reaching your goal of calling yourself an architect.

HOW TO USE THIS BOOK

This book contains 155 sample multiple-choice problems and three sample vignettes, as well as one complete practice exam consisting of 85 multiple-choice problems and three vignettes. These have been written to help you prepare for the Building Design & Construction Systems division of the Architect Registration Examination (ARE).

One of the best ways to prepare for the ARE is by solving sample problems. While you are studying for this division, use the sample problems in this book to make yourself familiar with the different types of problems and the breadth of topics you are likely to encounter on the actual exam. Then when it's time to take the ARE, you will already be comfortable with the format of the exam problems. Also, seeing which sample problems you can and cannot answer correctly will help you gauge your understanding of the topics covered in the Building Design & Construction Systems division.

The sample multiple-choice problems in this book are organized by subject area, so that you can concentrate on one subject at a time if you like. Each problem is immediately followed by its answer and an explanation.

Each sample vignette in this book can be solved directly on the base plan provided or on a sheet of tracing paper. Alternatively, you can download an electronic file of the base plan in PDF format from **www.ppi2pass.com/vignettes** for use in your own CAD program. (On the actual exam, vignettes are solved on the computer using NCARB's own software; see the Introduction for more information about this.) When you are finished with your solution to a vignette, compare it against the sample passing and failing solutions that follow. Individual target times are given for the vignettes in the Sample Problems section of this book, to give you an idea of how much time to budget for each one. On the actual exam (as in this book's practice exam), you will have a single period of time within which you must complete all three vignettes.

While the sample problems in this book are intended for you to use as you study for the exam, the practice exam is best used only when you have almost finished your study of the Building Design & Construction Systems topics. A week or two before you are scheduled to take the division, when you feel you are nearly ready for the exam, do a "dry run" by taking the practice exam in this book. This will hone your test-taking skills and give you a reality check about how prepared you really are.

The experience will be most valuable to you if you treat the practice exam as though it were an actual exam. Do not read the problems ahead of time and do not look at the solutions until after you've finished. Try to simulate the exam experience as closely as possible. This means locking yourself away in a quiet space, setting an alarm for the exam's testing time, and working through the entire practice exam with no coffee, television, or telephone—only your calculator, a pencil, your drafting tools or CAD program for the vignettes, and a few sheets of scratch paper. (On the actual exam, the CAD program, an on-screen calculator, scratch paper, and pencils are provided.) This will help you prepare to budget your time, give you an idea of what the actual exam experience will be like, and help you develop a test-taking strategy that works for you.

The target times for the two sections of the practice exam are

Multiple choice: 1.75 hours

Vignettes: 2.75 hours

Within the time allotted for each section, you may work on the problems or vignettes in any order and spend any amount of time on each one.

Record your answers for the multiple-choice section of the practice exam using the "bubble" answer form at the front of the exam. When you are finished, you can check your answers quickly against the filled-in answer key at the front of the Solutions section. Then turn to the solutions and read the explanations of the answers, especially those you answered incorrectly. The explanation will give you a better understanding of the intent of the problem and why individual options are right or wrong.

The Solutions section may also be used as a guide for the final phase of your studies. As opposed to a traditional study guide that is organized into chapters and paragraphs of facts, this problem-and-solution format can help you see how the exam might address a topic, and what types of problems you are likely to encounter. If you still are not clear about a particular subject after reading a solution's explanation, review the subject in one of your study resources. Give yourself time for further study, and then take the multiple-choice section again.

The vignette portions of the practice exam can be solved the same way as the sample vignettes, either directly on the base plans, on tracing paper, or with a CAD program using the electronic files downloaded from **www.ppi2pass.com/vignettes**. Try to solve all three vignettes within the target time given. When you are finished, compare your drawings against the passing and failing solutions given in the Solutions section.

This book is best used in conjunction with your primary study source or study guide, such as PPI's *ARE Review Manual*. *Building Design & Construction Systems: ARE Sample Problems and Practice Exam* is not intended to give you all the information you will need to pass this division of the ARE. Rather, it is designed to expose you to a variety of problem types and to help you sharpen your problem-solving and test-taking skills. With a sound review and the practice you'll get from this book, you'll be well on your way to successfully passing the Building Design & Construction Systems division of the Architect Registration Examination.

HOW SI UNITS ARE USED IN THIS BOOK

This book includes equivalent measurements in the text and illustrations using the Système International (SI), or the *metric system* as it is commonly called. However, the use of SI units for construction and book publishing in the United States is problematic. This is because the building construction industry in the United States (with the exception of federal construction) has generally not adopted the metric system. As a result, equivalent measurements of customary U.S. units (also called English or inch-pound units) are usually given as a *soft* conversion, in which customary U.S. measurements are simply converted into SI units using standard conversion factors. This always results in a number with excessive significant digits. When construction is done using SI units, the building is designed and drawn according to *hard* conversions, where planning dimensions and building products are based on a metric module from the beginning. For example, studs are spaced 400 mm on center to accommodate panel products that are manufactured in standard 1200 mm widths.

During the present time of transition to the Système International in the United States, code-writing bodies, federal laws such as the ADA and the ABA, product manufacturers, trade associations, and other construction-related industries typically still use the customary U.S. system and make soft conversions to develop SI equivalents. Some manufacturers produce the same products in sizes for each measuring system. Although there are industry standards for developing SI equivalents, there is no perfect consistency for rounding off when conversions are made. For example, the *International Building Code* shows a 152 mm equivalent when a 6 in dimension is required, while the *Americans with Disabilities Act and Architectural Barriers Act Accessibility Guidelines (ADA/ABA Guidelines)* give a 150 mm equivalent for the same customary U.S. dimension.

To further complicate matters, each book publisher may employ a slightly different house style in handling SI equivalents when customary U.S. units are used as the primary measuring system. The confusion is likely to continue until the United States construction industry adopts the SI system completely, eliminating the need for dual dimensioning in publishing.

For the purposes of this book, the following conventions have been adopted.

Throughout the book, the customary U.S. measurements are given first with the SI equivalent shown in parentheses. When the measurement is millimeters, units are not shown. For example, a dimension may be indicated as 4 ft 8 in (1422). When the SI equivalent is some other unit, such as for volume or area, the units are indicated. For example, 250 ft^2 (23 m^2).

Following standard conventions, all SI distance measurements in illustrations are in millimeters unless specifically indicated as meters.

When a measurement is given as part of a problem scenario, the SI measurement is not necessarily meant to be roughly equal to the U.S. measurement. For example, a hypothetical force on a beam might be given as 12 kips (12 kN). 12 kips is actually equal to about 53.38 kN, but the intention in such cases is only to provide two problems, one in U.S. units and one in SI units, of about the same difficulty. Solve the entire problem in either U.S. or SI units; don't try to convert from one to the other in the middle of solving a problem.

When dimensions are for informational use, the SI equivalent rounded to the nearest millimeter is used.

When dimensions are given and they relate to planning or design guidelines, the SI equivalent is rounded to the nearest 5 mm for numbers over a few inches and to the nearest 10 mm for numbers over a few feet. When the dimension exceeds several feet, the number is rounded to the nearest 100 mm. For example, if you need a space about 10 ft wide for a given activity, the modular, rounded SI equivalent will be given as 3000 mm. More exact conversions are not required.

When an item is only manufactured to a customary U.S. measurement, the nearest SI equivalent rounded to the nearest millimeter is given, unless the dimension is very small (as for metal gages), in which case a more precise decimal equivalent will be given. Some materials, such as glass, are often manufactured to SI sizes. So, for example, a nominal $^1/_2$ in thick piece of glass will have an SI equivalent of 13 mm but can be ordered as 12 mm.

When there is a hard conversion in the industry and an SI equivalent item is manufactured, the hard conversion is given. For example, a 24 × 24 ceiling tile would have the hard conversion of 600 × 600 (instead of 610) because these are manufactured and available in the United States.

When an SI conversion is used by a code, such as the *International Building Code*, or published in another regulation, such as the *ADA/ABA Guidelines*, the SI equivalents used by the issuing agency are printed in this book. For example, the same 10 ft dimension given previously as 3000 mm for a planning guideline would have an SI equivalent of 3048 mm in the context of the IBC because this is what that code requires. The *ADA/ABA Guidelines* generally follow the rounding rule, to take SI dimensions to the nearest 10 mm. For example, a 10 ft requirement for accessibility will be shown as 3050 mm. The code requirements for readers outside the United States may be slightly different.

This book uses different abbreviations for pounds of force and pounds of mass in customary U.S. units. The abbreviation used for pounds of force (pounds-force) is lbf, and the abbreviation used for pounds of mass (pounds-mass) is lbm.

CODES AND STANDARDS USED IN THIS BOOK

ACI 318-08: *Building Code Requirements for Structural Concrete*, 2008. American Concrete Institute, Farmington Hills, MI.

ADA/ABA Guidelines: *Americans with Disabilities Act and Architectural Barriers Act Accessibility Guidelines*, 2005. U.S. Architectural and Transportation Barriers Compliance Board, Washington, DC.

AISC: *Steel Construction Manual*, 13th ed., 2005. American Institute of Steel Construction, Chicago, IL.

ASTM Standard A36/A36M: *Standard Specification for Carbon Structural Steel*, 2008. American Society for Testing and Materials.

CSI: MasterFormat, 2010. Construction Specifications Institute, Alexandria, VA.

IBC: *International Building Code*, 2009. International Code Council, Washington, DC.

ICC/ANSI A117.1-2003: *Accessible and Usable Buildings and Facilities*, 2003. International Code Council. Washington, DC.

NFPA 10: *Standard for Portable Fire Extinguishers*, 2010. National Fire Protection Association, Quincy, MA.

NFPA 80: *Standard for Fire Doors and Other Opening Protectives*, 2010. National Fire Protection Association, Quincy, MA.

Safety Standard for Architectural Glazing Materials (CPSC 16 CFR 1201). Consumer Product Safety Commission.

The Secretary of the Interior's Standards for the Treatment of Historic Properties (37 CFR 68).

RECOMMENDED READING

General Reference

ARCOM. *MasterSpec*. Salt Lake City: ARCOM. (Familiarity with the format and language of specifications is very helpful.)

ARCOM and American Institute of Architects. *The Graphic Standards Guide to Architectural Finishes: Using MasterSpec to Evaluate, Select, and Specify Materials*. Hoboken, NJ: John Wiley & Sons.

Ballast, David Kent, and Steven E. O'Hara. *ARE Review Manual*. Belmont, CA: Professional Publications, Inc.

Fitch, James Marston. *Historic Preservation: Curatorial Management of the Built World*. Charlottesville: University Press of Virginia.

Guthrie, Pat. *Architect's Portable Handbook*. New York: McGraw-Hill.

Harris, Cyril M., ed. *Dictionary of Architecture and Construction*. New York: McGraw-Hill.

Mahoney, William D. *ADA/ABA Handbook: Accessibility Guidelines for Buildings and Facilities*. East Providence, RI: BNI Building News.

Ramsey, Charles G., and Harold R. Sleeper. *Architectural Graphic Standards*. Hoboken, NJ: John Wiley & Sons. (The student edition is an acceptable substitute for the professional version.)

U.S. Green Building Council. *LEED Reference Package for New Construction and Major Renovations*. Washington, DC: U.S. Green Building Council.

Building Design & Construction Systems

Allen, Edward. *Architectural Detailing: Function, Constructability, Aesthetics*. Hoboken, NJ: John Wiley & Sons.

Allen, Edward, and Joseph Iano. *Fundamentals of Building Construction: Materials and Methods*. Hoboken, NJ: John Wiley & Sons.

Ching, Francis D.K., and Cassandra Adams. *Building Construction Illustrated*. Hoboken, NJ: John Wiley & Sons.

McGowan, Maryrose, and Kelsey Kruse. *Interior Graphic Standards*. Hoboken, NJ: John Wiley & Sons.

Mendler, Sandra F., and William Odell. *The HOK Guidebook to Sustainable Design*. Hoboken, NJ: John Wiley & Sons.

Simmons, H. Leslie, and Harold B. Olin. *Construction: Principles, Materials, and Methods*. Hoboken, NJ: John Wiley & Sons.

Spiegel, Ross, and Dru Meadows. *Green Building Materials: A Guide to Product Selection and Specification*. Hoboken, NJ: John Wiley & Sons.

Tuluca, Adrian. *Energy Efficient Design and Construction for Commercial Buildings*. New York: McGraw-Hill.

Wakita, Osamu A., and Richard M. Linde. *The Professional Practice of Architectural Detailing*. Hoboken, NJ: John Wiley & Sons.

Graphic Vignettes

Allen, Edward, and Joseph Iano. *The Architect's Studio Companion: Rules of Thumb for Preliminary Design*. Hoboken, NJ: John Wiley & Sons.

Ambrose, James, and Peter Brandow. *Simplified Site Design*. Hoboken, NJ: John Wiley & Sons.

Ching, Francis D.K., and Steven R. Winkel. *Building Codes Illustrated: A Guide to Understanding the International Building Code*. Hoboken, NJ: John Wiley & Sons.

Hoke, John Ray, ed. *Architectural Graphic Standards*. Hoboken, NJ: John Wiley & Sons.

Karlen, Mark. *Space Planning Basics*. Hoboken, NJ: John Wiley & Sons.

Parker, Harry, John W. MacGuire, and James Ambrose. *Simplified Site Engineering*. Hoboken, NJ: John Wiley & Sons.

Architectural History

(Brush up on this before taking any of the multiple-choice exams, as architectural history problems are scattered throughout the sections.)

Curtis, William J.R. *Modern Architecture Since 1900*. London: Phaedon Press, Ltd.

Frampton, Kenneth. *Modern Architecture: A Critical History*. London: Thames and Hudson.

Trachtenberg, Marvin, and Isabelle Hyman. *Architecture: From Pre-History to Post-Modernism*. Englewood Cliffs, NJ: Prentice-Hall.

SAMPLE PROBLEMS

PRINCIPLES

1. Baker House dormitory at the Massachusetts Institute of Technology, designed by Alvar Aalto, represents which type of organizational scheme?

    A. radial
    B. linear
    C. clustered
    D. grid

Solution

Baker House Dormitory (1948) has a basically linear organization, even though it bends and curves along its length. The rooms were organized along a single corridor, with support spaces on the opposite sides of the corridor.

> *Study Note:* Be prepared for the occasional historical problem about the use of materials or other aspects of architectural design. Problems about notable architects and engineers and their use of materials and construction methods may also appear on the ARE.

The answer is B.

2. Selection of an earth-sheltered building design can be a representation of

    A. cost efficiency
    B. defensible space
    C. sustainability
    D. territoriality

Solution

Earth-sheltered buildings represent sustainability primarily because they are energy efficient and use low-cost, plentiful materials as part of their exterior covering.

> *Study Note:* Several problems on the ARE may involve somewhat subjective choices about the environmental and human context of material and building systems selection and detailing as they relate to social, cultural, psychological, and environmental issues.

The answer is C.

3. The honest expression of the nature of brick as a structural material is to utilize it

    A. to support horizontal lintels
    B. in barrel arches
    C. as a fine texture on large, flat walls
    D. in modular compositions

Solution

Brick is a compressive material with very little tensile or bending strength, so its basic nature would best suit it for use in compression applications, such as arches. Brick is also modular and creates a fine texture in large areas, but the question specifically refers to its use as a structural material.

The answer is B.

4. The Crystal Palace in London was the first building to utilize

     A. steel arches
     B. concrete ribbing
     C. large glass panels
     D. prefabricated iron parts

Solution

Prefabricated iron parts were first used to erect the Crystal Palace for the Great Exhibition of 1851. The use of standard prefabricated parts made it possible for the building to be dismantled and re-erected in a different location.

Although the Crystal Palace also made extensive use of glass, this was not the first use of large glass panels. Steel was not used in construction until later. Concrete ribbing was not used in the superstructure of the Crystal Palace.

The answer is D.

5. The concept of combining architecture with ecology to develop alternate urban habitats with greater density while using solar energy was advocated by

     A. Frank Lloyd Wright
     B. Kenzo Tange
     C. Le Corbusier
     D. Paolo Soleri

Solution

Paolo Soleri developed the concept of *arcology*, or the fusion of architecture with ecology, to develop ecological human "habitats" as an alternative to existing urban development. These habitats depend on population density to eliminate the need for automobiles in the city and are also located close to undeveloped land that can be used for raising food. One of Soleri's distinctive structural forms is the half dome, facing south to capture solar energy. His Arcosanti project in Arizona is a living laboratory of his ideas.

The answer is D.

6. What variable is used to measure the rate of heat transfer in any given thickness of material?

     A. conductivity
     B. coefficient of heat transmission
     C. resistance
     D. conductance

Solution

Conductivity is the amount of conductance for exactly 1 in (25) of material. Conductance is the amount of heat loss through a material of any thickness. Resistance is the amount of time it takes a certain amount of heat to pass through a material. The coefficient of heat transmission is the overall rate of heat flow.

The answer is D.

CODES AND REGULATIONS

7. When selecting a fire extinguisher cabinet, the most critical design feature is the

     A. projection distance from the wall
     B. size of the glazing
     C. height of the cabinet enclosure
     D. finish

Solution

The *ADA/ABA Guidelines* limit the projection of any construction element to a maximum of 4 in (100) from a wall when the element is located between 27 in (685) and 80 in (2030) above the floor. Because extinguisher cabinets fall within this range, they must be recessed or semi-recessed to meet the 4 in (100) requirement.

Glazing is not necessarily required, and if it is used there are no requirements for size. The height of the cabinet itself depends on what is installed within it. The type of finish is not critical. For example, painted stainless steel or bronze can be used. However, local jurisdictions may have requirements for the color and lettering type used for identification.

Study Note: In addition to meeting the 4 in (100) projection requirement, the height of the cabinet above the floor must also meet the ADA/ABA requirement of 48 in (1220) for unobstructed forward and side reach. National Fire Protection Association (NFPA) guidelines require that the maximum height to the top of a mounted cabinet be no more than 5 ft (1525) above the floor.

The answer is A.

8. An illustration of stair dimensions is shown.

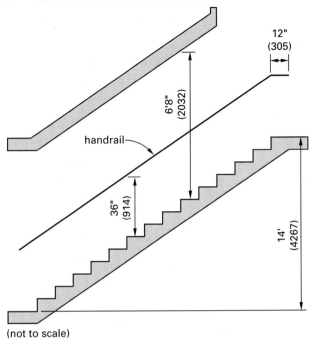

(not to scale)

According to model codes, which of the indicated stair dimensions is a code violation?

A. handrail height of 36 in (914)
B. headroom height of 6 ft 8 in (2032)
C. total rise height of 14 ft (4267)
D. handrail extension of 12 in (305)

Solution

The maximum allowable height between landings or floors (rise height) is 12 ft (3658). All of the other dimensions are correct. The height from the nosing to the top of a handrail must be between 34 in (864) and 38 in (965).

Study Note: Know all the required code and accessibility dimensions for ramps and stairs.

The answer is C.

9. What is the minimum length of the following toilet compartment at the end of a row of stalls, according to ICC/ANSI A117.1? The water closet is floor mounted.

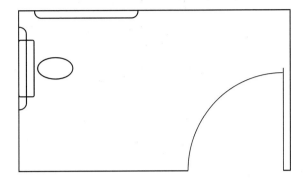

A. 90 in (2285)
B. 92 in (2335)
C. 95 in (2415)
D. 96 in (2440)

Solution

Section 604.8.2 of ICC/ANSI A117.1 states that the minimum clear floor space for a floor-mounted water closet is 60 in (1525) wide by 59 in (1500) long. The minimum space permitted at the door is 36 in (915).

In U.S. units:

$$59 \text{ in} + 36 \text{ in} = 95 \text{ in}$$

In SI units:

$$1500 \text{ mm} + 915 \text{ mm} = 2415 \text{ mm}$$

The answer is C.

10. According to model codes, the minimum width of an office exit corridor serving an occupant load of 55 is

A. 36 in (914)
B. 42 in (1067)
C. 44 in (1118)
D. 48 in (1219)

Solution

Model codes prescribe a minimum corridor width of 44 in (1118), with various exceptions. Corridors in residential occupancies or those serving an occupant load of less than 50 may be 36 in (914) wide. Other occupancies require wider corridors, but B occupancies (offices) require the 44 in (1118) width.

Study Note: Model codes also require that the minimum width of an exit corridor be calculated by multiplying the occupant load by a factor given in the codes, which varies depending on the occupancy, the interior area of the building, and whether the building is sprinklered. Both requirements must be checked, and the larger of the two should be used. If this calculation results in a number larger than other minimum requirements given in the code (such as for corridors), then the larger dimension must be used.

The answer is C.

11. What agency originally set requirements for safety glazing in buildings?

    A. ASTM International
    B. Consumer Product Safety Commission
    C. Glass Association of North America
    D. International Code Council

Solution

The Consumer Product Safety Commission originally set requirements for safety glazing, which are codified in the *Code of Federal Regulations*, CPSC 16 CFR 1201.

The answer is B.

12. According to model codes, interior finish requirements for woodwork are most stringent for

    A. recessed shelving
    B. cornice molding
    C. built-in furniture
    D. wainscoting

Solution

Model building codes regulate wainscoting as an interior finish material subject to a Class A, B, or C (sometimes called I, II, or III) flame spread rating, depending on occupancy, location in the building, and presence or absence of sprinklers. Since wainscoting could be restricted to a Class A flame spread rating, it is the most stringently regulated item listed.

Generally, codes do not regulate wood when it is used in furniture, shelving, molding, handrails, or other trim. Some codes only limit the flammability of wood trim to a Class C flame spread and limit the amount of trim to no more than 10% of the aggregate wall or ceiling area in which it is located.

The answer is D.

13. For accessible doors, the MINIMUM dimension of the distance x, as indicated in the drawing, is ____ in (mm). (Fill in the blank.)

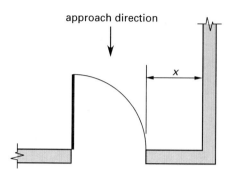

Solution

For a front approach to an in-swinging door (pull side), there must be a minimum of 18 in (445) on the latch side of the door. For an out-swinging door (push side), 12 in (305) are required on the latch side of the door.

    Study Note: Know some of the fundamental dimensions required for accessibility, such as turnaround area, toilet room dimensions, maneuvering clearances at doors, and reach heights.

The answer is 18 in (445).

14. A fire-rated gypsum board partition must always consist of

    A. Type X gypsum board
    B. full-height construction
    C. attachment according to testing laboratory standards
    D. all of the above

Solution

Fire-rated partitions must be constructed according to tested and approved methods that include using Type X gypsum board, the method of attachment to the framing, how the joints are finished, the type and size of studs, and other details. In addition, the fire separation must extend from the slab to the rated slab above, not just to a suspended, finish ceiling.

The answer is D.

15. What is the building code requirement for pairs of exit doors with astragals?

    A. weather stripping
    B. door stop
    C. coordinator
    D. flush bolts

Solution

A coordinator prevents the door leaf with the astragal from closing before the other leaf, so the pair of doors seals properly.

The answer is C.

16. How much fire protection-rated glazing (wire glass) is permitted in a $1\frac{1}{2}$-hour rated door in an exterior wall?

    A. 100 in^2 (645 cm^2)
    B. 1296 in^2 (8362 cm^2)
    C. The amount of glazing is not limited.
    D. No glazing is permitted.

Solution

According to the IBC, Table 715.5.4, no glazing is permitted in a $1\frac{1}{2}$-hour rated door in an exterior wall.

All glazing in fire-rated doors must be either $\frac{1}{4}$ in (6.35) wire glass or ceramic glazing. This problem addresses only wire glass. A $1\frac{1}{2}$-hour rated door that is not in an exterior wall is permitted to have 100 in^2 (645 cm^2) of glazing. A $\frac{3}{4}$-hour rated door may have 1296 in^2 (8362 cm^2) of glazing per leaf. The amount of glazing is not limited in a 20-minute rated door.

Ceramic glazing must comply with NFPA 80, *Standard for Fire Doors and Other Opening Protectives*.

The answer is D.

17. Which of the following is NOT a requirement of NFPA 10, *Standard for Portable Fire Extinguishers*?

    A. Fire extinguisher cabinets must have a vision panel or be clearly marked with a sign.
    B. Fire extinguishers must be tested regularly and have an approved label.
    C. Fire extinguisher cabinets may not protrude into the hallway more than 4 in (102).
    D. When fire extinguishers are required, no occupant may be more than 75 ft (22.9 m) from a fire extinguisher.

Solution

NFPA 10, *Standard for Portable Fire Extinguishers* is referenced in many codes to provide additional requirements for this type of fire-suppression system. When required, extinguishers must be clearly marked and visible; located no more than 75 ft (22.9 m) from each building occupant; properly maintained, tested, and labeled; and readily accessible in case of an emergency.

A fire extinguisher cabinet must not protrude more than 4 in (102) into the hallway, but this is a requirement of the *ADA/ABA Guidelines*, not NFPA.

The answer is C.

18. A grocery store parking lot has 100 parking spaces. According to the *ADA/ABA Guidelines*, at least ____ accessible spaces must be provided. (Fill in the blank.)

Solution

According to the *ADA/ABA Guidelines*, the ratio of accessible parking spaces to total parking spaces is 1:25 up to 200 spaces, with an additional accessible space for each additional 100 parking spaces up to 500. Above 500 spaces, accessible spaces are determined as a percentage of the total parking spaces provided.

Local zoning ordinances or codes may differ from ADA/ABA recommendations, so all applicable guidelines should be consulted.

The answer is 4.

19. What does it mean when a building material is non-combustible?

    A. It will not ignite and burn when subjected to fire.
    B. It will withstand flame impingement.
    C. It will not readily spread fire once ignited.
    D. It has a minimum 1-hour fire rating.

Solution

A noncombustible building material will not ignite and burn when subjected to fire.

The answer is A.

20. Restrictions on surface finishes in all model codes are based primarily on

    A. occupancy and construction type
    B. occupant load and location in the building
    C. location in the building and occupancy
    D. occupancy group and sprinklering

Solution

The primary restrictions on surface finishes given in model codes (such as in IBC Table 803.5) are the occupancy group and the location in the building according to exiting requirements. Having a building with a sprinkler system only modifies the basic requirements and allows the required flame-spread rating to be dropped one class in some instances.

The answer is C.

21. Construction type refers to the

    A. major materials used to construct a building
    B. fire-resistance ratings of various building components
    C. maximum area and height of a building
    D. use of a building and fire-protection methods used

Solution

The hourly ratings of major building components, such as the structural frame, bearing walls, exterior walls, floor structure, and roof structure, together determine the construction type according to Tables 601 and 602 in the IBC.

The answer is B.

22. What is the minimum clear width for an accessible door?

    A. 30 in (760)
    B. 32 in (815)
    C. 34 in (865)
    D. 36 in (915)

Solution

According to the *ADA/ABA Guidelines*, a door that is required to be accessible must have a minimum clear width of 32 in (815). For a hinged door, this is measured with the door open to 90 degrees; a folding or sliding door is measured when fully open.

The answer is B.

23. In surveying an existing corridor to see if it met accessibility guidelines, an architect discovers the following two items that are questionable.

I. a small fire-hose cabinet extending 5 in (127) from the wall
II. a $^1/_4$ in (6) high threshold below a pair of normally open doors

Which item must be modified to make the corridor barrier-free?

    A. neither I nor II
    B. I but not II
    C. II but not I
    D. both I and II

Solution

No objects greater than 4 in (100) can protrude into an accessible route if the lower edge of the object is greater than 27 in (685) above the floor. It is reasonable to assume that a small fire-hose cabinet would have its lower edge higher than this distance, so it would be limited to a maximum 4 in (100) protrusion. Therefore, item I would have to be modified. Any change in level of $^1/_4$ in (6) or less does not require any edge treatment, so item II would not have to be modified.

The answer is B.

SITE PLANNING AND DESIGN

24. A soils report has indicated that the water table is 5 ft 0 in (1500) above the basement level of a planned three-story building. What type of construction technique will most likely be required?

    A. dampproofing
    B. surcharging
    C. waterproofing
    D. waterstopping

Solution

Waterproofing is the control of water and moisture that is subject to hydrostatic pressure. It can refer to the application of watertight membranes, waterstops, or bentonite panels when building below the water table.

Dampproofing is the control of water and moisture when hydrostatic pressure is not present. *Surcharging* is the preloading of the ground with fill material to cause consolidation and settlement of the underlying soil. Surcharging is used to increase the bearing capacity of soil or to decrease possible settlement, or both. A *waterstop* is a preformed piece of material used to seal construction joints. Although waterstops would be used in this situation, they are a subset of the larger requirement to waterproof the entire basement slab and a portion of the basement walls.

The answer is C.

---

25. A building with a basement is being designed in a wet climate. Which of the following water-control materials and/or methods should the architect recommend for the foundation and basement walls?

I. cementitious coatings
II. geotextiles
III. French drains
IV. sloping soil away from the building

    A. II and III only
    B. III and IV only
    C. I, II, and IV only
    D. II, III, and IV only

Solution

Geotextiles, French drains, and sloping soil away from the building would all be appropriate means of draining water from a building in a wet climate or where groundwater was present.

Item I is incorrect because cementitious coatings are only used for dampproofing, and if they were used the other three choices would also have to be used.

> *Study Note:* Understand the various types of dampproofing and waterproofing. For dampproofing these include admixtures for concrete, bituminous coatings, cementitious coatings, membranes, and plastics for dampproofing. For waterproofing these include elastomeric membranes, liquid-applied membranes, and bentonite panels.

The answer is D.

---

26. A deep excavation for a high-rise building in an urban area would require

    A. battered walls
    B. needle beams
    C. steel sheeting
    D. tiebacks

Solution

A deep excavation would require the use of vertical soldier beams supporting horizontal timber breast boards or cribbing. The vertical soldier beams must be anchored into the adjacent earth with grouted tieback rods. Even steel sheeting would require tiebacks for support.

A battered wall is simply a type of retaining wall using a material, such as stones or brick, slightly angled to support the adjacent earth. It is not appropriate for a deep excavation wall in an urban area where space is limited. Needle beams are used to temporarily support a structure when its foundation is repaired or deepened. Steel sheeting requires the use of rakers that extend into the excavation site, limiting the depth of the excavation and interfering with construction activities in the excavated area.

> *Study Note:* Know the basic terminology of shoring and excavation.

The answer is D.

---

27. A soils report indicates that bentonite is present below the site of a proposed two-story manufacturing building. What type of foundation system should be used?

    A. drilled piers with grade beams
    B. raft foundation
    C. caissons with pile caps
    D. extended spread footings

Solution

Bentonite is an expansive type of clay that can push foundations and floor slabs upward when it gets wet. To prevent this, drilled piers are used to support the building weight on bedrock or stable soil below the bentonite. Grade beams span continuously between the piers and transmit building loads from the superstructure to the piers. Voids are left below the grade beams to allow the bentonite to expand without transmitting uplift forces.

A raft foundation is used to distribute a building load over a large area of low-bearing capacity soil. Caissons with pile caps are used to distribute a load from one column to two or more caissons or piers and would only be appropriate if there was a void below the pile cap. Spread footings placed on bentonite would be subject to the uplift of the swelling clay soil and would not be appropriate.

The answer is A.

28. Which of the following pedestrian walk materials provides the best positive grade-level drainage away from a building?

    A. asphaltic concrete

    B. brick pavers

    C. cobblestones

    D. concrete

Solution

A safe pedestrian walk should not have a slope exceeding $^{1}/_{4}$ in/ft (20 mm/m) perpendicular to the direction of travel. This allows for drainage without creating a dangerous cross slope. Of the materials listed, concrete could be finished to provide a continuous, uniform slope for drainage in conjunction with a smooth walking surface.

Asphalt could be used, but it is more difficult to smooth uniformly at such a low slope. Minor dips and surface irregularities in the asphalt might cause ponding of water against or toward the building. Both brick pavers and cobblestone would allow water to seep into the joints near the building.

The answer is D.

29. For a large building being planned with a two-level basement used for meeting rooms, which of these water-related soil problems would be the most important to solve?

    A. uplift pressure on the lowest slab

    B. moisture penetration caused by hydrostatic pressure

    C. deterioration of foundation insulation

    D. reduced load-carrying capacity of the soil

Solution

All of the answer options listed would need to be addressed, but because the question asks which is *most* important, a judgment call is required. Option D is unlikely because a large building would probably utilize piers or caissons for the foundation, so the load-carrying capacity of the soil would not be as critical. Foundation insulation could be easily selected to avoid deterioration problems, so option C is an unlikely answer. Of the two remaining answers, hydrostatic pressure could cause the most problems, so this is the primary problem to be solved.

The answer is B.

30. If a soil is analyzed as being primarily silty, how should it be characterized?

    A. very fine material of organic matter

    B. rigid particles with moderately high bearing capacity

    C. particles with some cohesion and plasticity in their behavior

    D. smaller particles with occasional plastic behavior

Solution

Option A describes organic material, option B describes gravels, and option C describes clays.

The answer is D.

31. In the partial plan of a concrete basement shown, what would be the best way to improve the economy of the concrete formwork?

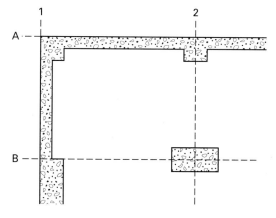

    A. Make the column square.

    B. Separate the pilaster at A2 from the wall.

    C. Form the pilaster at A1 with a diagonal.

    D. Make the wall along grid line 1 a uniform thickness.

Solution

Forming corners in concrete always adds to the cost, so making the wall a uniform thickness would be most economical even though more concrete would be required. Making the column square would decrease the amount of concrete but would still require the same amount of forming. Separating the pilaster from the wall would actually increase the cost of formwork. Forming the pilaster with a diagonal would not be appropriate because of the structural problems caused by decreasing the column area and placing reinforcement.

The answer is D.

32. In the illustration shown, what is the purpose of the gravel?

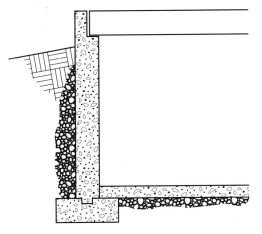

A. to reduce hydrostatic pressure
B. to keep the soil from direct contact with the concrete
C. to provide a firm base for concrete bearing
D. to hold the membrane in place and protect it

Solution

The gravel provides open spaces for any water under hydrostatic pressure to lose its pressure and drip to drains near the footing. Although it does this by preventing direct contact of the soil with the wall, preventing contact is not the sole purpose.

The answer is A.

33. Which of the following building areas is excluded from a calculation of the architectural area of a building?

A. a mechanical penthouse with 6 ft (1.8 m) headroom
B. an open courtyard
C. a duct shaft
D. a porch

Solution

The architectural area of a building is the sum of the areas of all of the floors. However, certain spaces within the building are treated differently from others for the purposes of this calculation. Some are excluded entirely, such as courtyards and other open areas like fire escapes and exterior stairs. Others, such as rooms with less than 6 ft (1.8 m) of headroom and porches, are multiplied by 0.5.

A full description of the methods of calculating the areas of spaces is available in the *Architect's Handbook of Professional Practice*, and a summary can be found in *Architectural Graphic Standards*.

The answer is B.

MATERIAL COSTS

34. Which of the following factors accounts for the highest cost of a lighting system over time?

A. lamps
B. luminaires
C. installation
D. operation

Solution

Over the life cycle of a lighting system, the continuing operating cost for electricity is the single largest expense. For nonresidential applications, maintenance (such as the replacement of lamps and cleaning of luminaires) is the second greatest expense.

The answer is D.

35. Which of the following installed suspended ceiling systems is the least expensive?

A. concealed spline set in a grid with 12 in by 12 in (300 by 300) mineral-fiber tiles
B. gypsum wallboard attached to furring channels attached to $1^{1}/_{2}$ in (38) cold-rolled channels
C. metal pan with acoustic pads set in 2 ft by 2 ft (600 by 600) exposed grids
D. mineral board tiles set in 2 ft by 4 ft (600 by 1200) exposed grids

Solution

Of the choices listed, a standard 2 ft by 4 ft (600 by 1200) exposed grid with mineral fiber ceiling tile is the least expensive. It is followed, in increasing order of cost, by gypsum wallboard, concealed spline mineral fiber, and metal pan with acoustic pads.

Study Note: Problems related to material costs and construction methods generally ask one of two questions: "Which is the least expensive?" or "Which is the most expensive?" Although you do not need to know specific costs, you should have a general idea of the *relative* costs of similar materials and systems.

The answer is D.

36. Which of the following wood flooring types has the lowest material cost?

     A.   maple strip over sleepers
     B.   oak strip, no. 1 common
     C.   oak plank
     D.   white oak parquet

Solution

Oak strip flooring is one of the least expensive wood flooring types. White oak parquet and oak plank are the most expensive.

The answer is B.

37. Which of the following door frame materials would provide the greatest durability at the lowest possible cost?

     A.   aluminum
     B.   hollow metal
     C.   stainless steel
     D.   wood (e.g., oak)

Solution

A wood frame would be the least expensive option but would not provide the same durability as a metal door frame. Of the metal door frames listed, standard hollow metal (steel) would be the least expensive.

Study Note: Although most problems regarding costs of materials and methods are objective, some may require a judgment call or the setting of priorities.

The answer is B.

38. Which of the following wall coverings has the highest material cost?

     A.   acrylic glazed coating
     B.   cork tile
     C.   commercial-grade grass cloth
     D.   medium-weight vinyl wallcovering

Solution

Cork tile is the most expensive material listed. Acrylic glazed coatings have the lowest cost of those listed, followed by medium-weight vinyl wallcovering and grass cloth.

The answer is B.

CONCRETE

39. Which of these statements about reinforcing bar (rebar) sizes is FALSE?

     A.   American and metric sizes are now based on a unitless number.
     B.   American bar numbers equal the number of eighths of an inch across the diameter.
     C.   Soft metric numbers approximately equal the diameter in millimeters.
     D.   Hard metric numbers are based on the cross-sectional area in square millimeters.

Solution

The designation system for American standard sizes of rebar is based on the number of eighths of an inch in the nominal diameter of a bar, up to 1 in.

The soft metric sizes are based on the approximate number of millimeters in the nominal diameter. For example, a no. 5 bar in the American designation is $^5/_8$ in, which in soft metric is 15.9 mm or a no. 16 bar. In hard metric, the actual size is different, and the numbering system is based on round numbers of the cross-sectional area, using the letter "M" as a suffix. For example, the nearest size to an American no. 5 bar is a 15M with an area of 200 mm².

The answer is A.

40. One nondestructive test used to measure the strength of concrete after it has hardened in its final form is the

     A.   core cylinder test
     B.   cylinder test
     C.   impact hammer test
     D.   Kelly ball test

Solution

The impact hammer test involves snapping a spring-loaded plunger against a concrete surface and measuring the amount of rebound. The amount of rebound gives an approximate reading of concrete strength.

A cylinder test requires that a sample be taken at the time the concrete is poured, before it has hardened. A core cylinder test can give the strength of hardened concrete, but the test is destructive to the concrete, and the sample needs to be tested in a laboratory. Both the core cylinder test and the Kelly ball test require the use of fresh concrete.

Study Note: Problems on the various types of concrete tests are common on the ARE. Review the following tests: slump test, cylinder test, core cylinder test, Kelly ball test, K-slump test, and impact hammer test.

There are also tests that measure the moisture in concrete. These tests are meant for slabs that are to receive moisture-sensitive finishes. They include the following.

- *polyethylene sheet test:* This test uses a plastic sheet taped tightly to a concrete floor. After 16 hours the underside of the plastic is inspected for moisture.

- *electrical resistance test:* This test determines moisture by measuring the electrical conductivity of the concrete between the meter probes.

- *quantitative calcium chloride test:* This test uses a quantity of calcium chloride sealed under a plastic dome placed on the concrete for 60 to 72 hours. The amount of moisture the chloride absorbs is mathematically converted to a moisture emission expressed in pounds per 1000 ft^2 per 24 hour period (grams per mm^2 per 24 hour period).

- *hygrometer test* or *relative humidity test:* This test determines moisture emission by measuring the relative humidity of the atmosphere confined adjacent to the concrete floor.

The answer is C.

41.   If too much water is placed in a concrete mix, which of the following problems might develop?

   A.   laitance
   B.   efflorescence
   C.   hydration
   D.   segregation

Solution

Laitance is a surface deposit of low-strength material containing cement and fine aggregates (sand) brought to the surface of concrete. It is caused by having too much water in the concrete mix, which results in water bleeding to the top.

Efflorescence is a white, crystalline deposit of water-soluble salts on the surface of masonry and sometimes concrete. It is caused when water seeps into the masonry and dissolves soluble salts, which are brought to the surface. When the water evaporates, the salts are left on the surface. *Hydration* is simply the chemical process of the hardening of concrete when water mixes with cement. *Segregation* is the separation of the constituent parts of the concrete when the concrete is either dropped too far or moved excessively in the horizontal direction while it is being placed.

The answer is A.

42.   A section of a precast concrete panel attached to a cast-in-place concrete structure is shown.

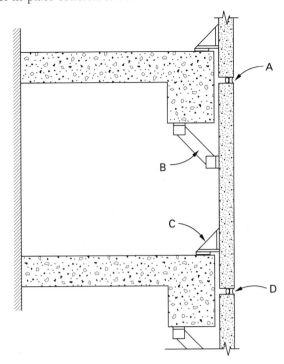

Which connection point should allow for both vertical and lateral movement?

   A.   point A
   B.   point B
   C.   point C
   D.   point D

Solution

A precast panel should have only two points of bearing on the structure. These are indicated at point C. One point should be a rigid connection and the other should provide for lateral movement. The remaining points of connection to the structure, or tiebacks as they are often called, should allow for both vertical and lateral movement of the panel due to differential movement of the structure and panel, and due to expansion and contraction caused by temperature differences.

The answer is B.

43. Which of the concrete joints shown connects two successive pours of concrete?

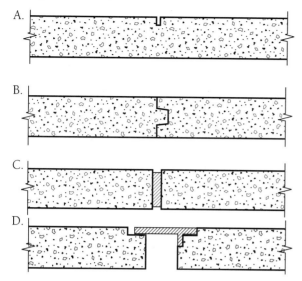

Solution

Option B shows a construction joint, which would be used to physically connect a new pour of concrete to a previously poured section. In most cases the two sections are connected with a keyed joint. Reinforcing bars across the joint are also commonly used.

The drawing in option A shows a control joint. Option C shows an isolation joint, which can be used for successive pours of concrete but does not *connect* the two pairs. Option D shows an expansion joint used to allow two sections of a building to move independently.

The answer is B.

44. Expansion joints in concrete walks should be located at a maximum spacing of

    A. 5 ft
    B. 10 ft
    C. 20 ft
    D. 25 ft

Solution

Control joints placed where separate sections of concrete are poured and in walks are placed 5 ft (1500) apart. Expansion joints with a joint filler are placed a maximum of 20 ft (6100) apart.

The answer is C.

45. When the architect is on the job observing concrete placement, what is most likely to be of LEAST concern?

    A. height of a bottom-dump bucket above the forms as the concrete is being placed
    B. type of vibrator being used
    C. location of the rebar in relation to the forms
    D. method of support of the forms

Solution

The height of the dump bucket is important because dropping concrete too far causes segregation, which should not be allowed. The location of rebar is important because of the minimum coverages required to protect the steel from moisture. The method of form support is important because unstable forms can affect the final appearance and size of the concrete. They can also be a safety hazard, but this is the contractor's responsibility.

The answer is B.

46. What cement would be used in slip form construction?

    A. Type I
    B. Type II
    C. Type III
    D. Type IV

Solution

Type III cement is high-early-strength—the type needed for rapid slip form construction. Type I is normal cement. Type II is low heat and sulfate resistant, and Type IV is slow setting and low heat for massive structures.

The answer is C.

47. What is used to minimize corner chipping of concrete?

    A. chamfer strips
    B. hardeners
    C. rustication strips
    D. walers

Solution

A *chamfer strip* is a small, triangular piece of material placed in the corners for forms to prevent sharp 90° corners, which are difficult to cast and have a tendency to break off during use or when the forms are removed.

The answer is A.

48. What is the primary purpose of the voids in a cored slab?

    A. to allow electrical services to be concealed in the slab

    B. to make a more efficient load-carrying member

    C. to make erection easier

    D. to minimize weight

Solution

As with any beam, the deeper the member, the more efficient the beam. Using a cored slab rather than a solid slab allows the depth to be increased without increasing the weight in the center of the beam where it is not needed. Options A and D are partially correct, but option B is the best choice.

The answer is B.

49. Which of the vertical joints shown would be appropriate for a concrete basement wall?

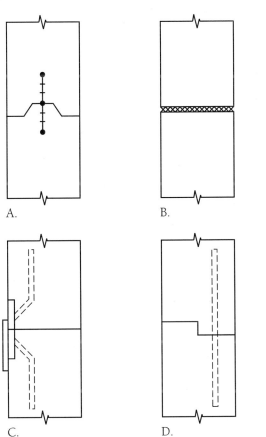

A.   B.

C.   D.

Solution

Option A shows a strong keyed joint with a waterstop to prevent water penetration. The other selections show joints that are weak structurally or that do not provide for adequate waterproofing.

The answer is A.

50. At what temperature do workers need to take steps to protect concrete when cold weather is predicted?

    A. 0°F (−18°C)

    B. 32°F (0°C)

    C. 40°F (4°C)

    D. 45°F (78°C)

Solution

Construction operations generally discontinue or switch from regular activity to cold-weather mode at 40°F (4°C). A concrete pour can proceed at temperatures below 40°F (4°C). However, the water and sand must be heated to ensure that none of the constituents have frozen, and the concrete must be heated for at least seven days after placement, during the early curing stage.

Other temperature-sensitive materials, such as sealants, should not be applied when the mercury dips below 40°F (4°C).

The answer is C.

51. When specifying small batches of concrete, what does a 1:2:5 mix mean?

    A. 1 part cement, 2 parts sand, and 5 parts coarse aggregate

    B. 1 part coarse aggregate, 2 parts sand, and 5 parts cement

    C. 1 part water, 2 parts cement, and 5 parts aggregate

    D. 1 part cement, 2 parts water, and 5 parts aggregate

Solution

Concrete mixes specified by volume follow the standard nomenclature of three values expressed in proportion to one another. The first number expresses the proportion of cement; the middle number expresses the proportion of fine aggregate (sand); and the last number expresses the proportion of coarse aggregate (gravel). The amount of water to be added to the mix is not included in the mix ratio.

The answer is A.

52. Which of the following statements is FALSE?

    A. Type III cement (high-early-strength) is often used for precast concrete members.

    B. Precast concrete members can be a maximum of 14 ft (4.3 m) wide.

    C. Concrete used in precast members is typically 3000 psi (20 684 kPa).

    D. Conditions are more controlled during the production of precast concrete members than they would be for similar structural systems built in the field.

Solution

Concrete used in precast members is generally a higher-strength mix than the 3000 psi (20 684 kPa) concrete typically used for site cast applications.

Type III (high-early-strength) cement and steam curing allows prestress plants to get finished beams and tees out of the beds and into the yard more quickly so that production can continue. They are then warehoused in the yard until they have passed 28-day cylinder testing.

Precast members are generally transported over the highway, so their width is limited to the width of a travel lane.

In general, conditions can be better controlled during the production of precast concrete than they can in the field. Forms can be used repeatedly, and curing can take place under shelter and in controlled conditions, making precast concrete products both economical and consistent.

The answer is C.

MASONRY

53. Which type of masonry cement mortar has the highest compressive strength?

    A. Type M
    B. Type N
    C. Type O
    D. Type S

Solution

Type M mortar has a minimum average 28-day compressive strength of 2500 psi (17.2 MPa). Type O has the lowest compressive strength, 350 psi (2.4 MPa).

Study Note: For exterior walls and interior walls under normal loads, Type N mortar is commonly used. Type S mortar is used for heavier loading on interior walls and for exterior walls at or below grade, such as foundation walls, retaining walls, pavements, walks, and patios. When high-strength mortar is required for heavy loads or for cases where the mortar will be exposed to severe, saturated freezing, Type S or M mortar is used. Type O mortar is used only for light loads and where freezing is not expected.

The answer is A.

54. Which of the following orientations is used in a soldier course of brick? (Shading sides face forward.)

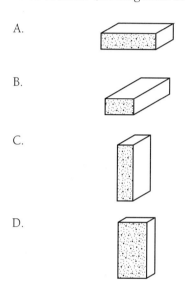

A.

B.

C.

D.

Solution

Option C is used in a soldier course of brick.

Option A is used in a stretcher course of brick. Option B is used in a header course. Option D is used in a sailor course.

Study Note: Know the various types of brick courses, bonding patterns, and mortar joints, especially the mortar joints that give maximum protection against weathering and water penetration (concave).

Terms to Know

collar joint: the vertical joint between masonry withes

The answer is C.

55. In masonry walls, water is prevented from seeping back into the wall through capillary action by using

    A. base flashing

    B. coping

    C. drips

    D. weep holes

Solution

Drips are extensions of through-wall flashing or projections below masonry units that extend beyond the primary plane of the wall. The purpose of a drip is to force water that is draining off flashing or a sill to fall down and away from the wall rather than to adhere to the wall and possibly flow back into the wall through capillary action or cracks below the flashing.

The question asks for the solution that will prevent water from seeping back into the wall, so it can be assumed that the water is already outside, precluding options A and D. Option B is incorrect because coping simply covers a parapet and may include drips.

> *Study Note:* Study the basic components of masonry construction, including multi-wythe construction, flashing, reinforcing, opening details, and connections to backup walls or the superstructure. Also know the methods of repairing masonry walls and grout for renovations.

The answer is C.

56. Under wind pressures of 20 psf (958 Pa), the maximum area allowed for individual exterior wall panels using standard unit glass block is _____ ft² (m²). (Fill in the blank.)

Solution

A standard unit glass block is hollow and has a specified thickness of $3^7/8$ in (98). Model codes limit the areas of the individual exterior wall panels using this glass block to 144 ft² (13.4 m²).

Solid unit glass block is limited to 100 ft² (9.3 m²) for both interior and exterior walls. Interior standard unit glass block walls are limited to 250 ft² (23.2 m²).

The answer is 144 ft² (13.4 m²).

57. According to most building codes, horizontal masonry reinforcement is required every

    A. 8.0 in (200)

    B. 16 in (400)

    C. 24 in (600)

    D. 32 in (800)

Solution

Most building codes require horizontal reinforcement in both brick and concrete masonry walls a minimum of every 16 in (400). The reinforcing may be a continuous truss or ladder type laid in the mortar joints.

The answer is B.

58. Which mortar type has the highest compressive strength?

    A. M

    B. N

    C. O

    D. S

Solution

Type M masonry has a compressive strength of 2500 psi (17 237 kPa). Types S and N have strengths of 1800 psi (12 411 kPa) and 750 psi (5171 kPa), respectively, and Type O is the lowest with a compressive strength of 350 psi (2413 kPa).

The answer is A.

59. What type of brick would most likely be specified for an eastern exposure in New Hampshire?

    A. NW

    B. FBX

    C. MW

    D. SW

Solution

SW stands for severe weathering and would be the type that should be specified for the northeastern United States. NW is normal weathering, and MW is moderate weathering. FBX refers to the finish appearance.

The answer is D.

60. Which area in the masonry wall assembly shown would be most susceptible to water penetration?

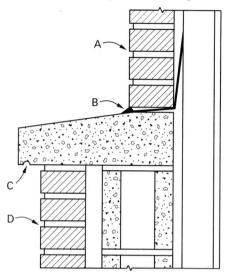

Solution

A raked joint like that shown in the masonry wall above the ledge (area A) is not a good one to use because water running down the wall can seep into the joint by capillary action. The details at areas B and C are correctly executed. The flashing and sealant at area B would keep water out, and the drip at area C would prevent water from running under the ledge and into the masonry joint at area D.

The answer is A.

61. Three courses of a bull stretcher using a standard brick and standard mortar joints equal

    A.   8 in (200)
    B.   12 in (300)
    C.   15 in (375)
    D.   18 in (450)

Solution

A *bull stretcher* is a brick laid on its face so that the width of the brick is visible. With a width of $3^5/_8$ in (90) and a mortar joint of $^3/_8$ in (10), three courses would be 12 in (300). Three *standard stretcher* courses equal 8 in (200).

The answer is B.

62. If cracking occurred along the joints of a brick wall in a generally diagonal direction from a window corner up to the top of the wall, which of the following would most likely be the cause?

    A.   lack of vertical control joints
    B.   horizontal reinforcement placed too far apart
    C.   poor grouting of the cavity
    D.   inadequate mortar

Solution

Vertical cracking is usually an indication that the brick wall is not able to move laterally, which is a condition caused by lack of vertical expansion joints.

The answer is A.

63. What is the most important fire-resistance property of a CMU partition?

    A.   overall width
    B.   density
    C.   joint reinforcement
    D.   equivalent thickness

Solution

Concrete masonry partitions are usually hollow, so the actual thickness of the solid material, not the actual overall width, is used to rate the fire resistance of the unit.

The answer is D.

64. What is a requirement for a door opening in a masonry partition?

    A.   bond beam
    B.   arch action
    C.   weep holes
    D.   flashing

Solution

A bond beam is a masonry unit made to accommodate reinforcing and grout to span openings in masonry walls. These are often used in place of steel lintels.

The answer is A.

65.   Which of the following statements is true?

A.   Spalling occurs when water-soluble salts in masonry units or mortar leach out of the brick.

B.   Tuck pointing is used to finish mortar joints during construction of a new brick wall.

C.   Flashing in a masonry wall should be terminated just before the face of the brick for best appearance.

D.   A concealed flashing in a masonry wall with a concrete backup should terminate in a reglet.

Solution

Reglets are horizontal grooves cast into concrete that allow a piece of flashing to be slipped inside and then carried across the airspace and through the brick for proper drainage and moisture control.

Efflorescence (not spalling) occurs when salts leach out of a masonry assembly. This produces a white powdery substance that stains the face of the brick.

Tuck pointing is a process used to repair failing mortar joints. It involves removing the deteriorated mortar to a certain depth and inserting new, compatible mortar into the space, then striking it with a new, water-resistant edge treatment.

Flashing should always be extended at least $^3/_4$ in (19) beyond the face of the brick and turned down at a 45° angle for proper drainage. If the flashing is terminated before the face of the brick, the moisture will seep into the brick and mortar and can cause damage. The 45° bend provides a drip edge that leads the moisture away from the face of the brick.

The answer is D.

66.   Identify the following brick bond.

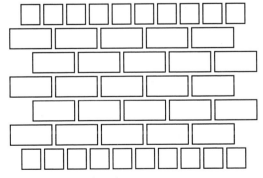

A.   common bond
B.   running bond
C.   English bond
D.   Flemish bond

Solution

The brick bond shown is a common bond. It consists of a header course, five (or more) courses of running bond, and another header course. The pattern then repeats for the height of the wall. Traditionally, in a double-wythe brick wall, the header course "locked" the two wythes together.

The answer is A.

METALS

67.   What is the designation for the most commonly used structural steel for beams?

A.   A36
B.   A153
C.   A441
D.   A501

Solution

A36 steel refers to the American Society for Testing and Materials (ASTM) Standard A36/A36M, *Standard Specification for Carbon Structural Steel*. Steel meeting this standard has a minimum yield point of 36,000 psi (250 MPa). A36 is one of the commonly used steels for riveted, bolted, and welded construction of bridges and buildings and for general structural purposes.

A153 is the standard for hot-dip zinc coating (hot-dip) on iron and steel hardware. A441 steel is a high-strength structural steel used for welded construction. A501 is the designation for hot-formed welded and seamless carbon steel structural tubing.

The answer is A.

68.   Which of the following is NOT a standard designation for open-web steel joists?

A.   DLH
B.   K
C.   LH
D.   ML

Solution

DLH is the designation for deep long-span joists. K is the designation for standard open-web joists, and LH is the designation for long-span joists.

Study Note: The depths in the K series range from 8 in (200) to 30 in (750) and increase in 2 in (50) increments. The depths in the LH and DLH series range from 18 in (460) to 96 in (2440) and increase in 4 in (100) increments.

The answer is D.

69.   The stringers of prefabricated steel utility stairs are normally constructed of

    A. angle iron
    B. channel sections
    C. steel plate
    D. tube sections

Solution

Although any of the listed forms can be used, the stringers are *normally* constructed of steel channel sections with the flanges turned away from the stair. The steel treads and risers are welded to the webs of the sections.

Study Note: Understand the basic construction of various miscellaneous metal fabrications such as steel stairs, spiral stairs, ladders, handrails, and railings.

The answer is B.

70.   In the detail shown, the purpose of the item labeled x is to

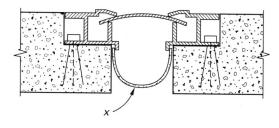

    A. allow for vertical movement
    B. collect condensation
    C. provide a fire rating
    D. create a sound seal

Solution

The detail shows a building separation joint at the floor line. Fire protection is provided by one or more layers of fire-resistive material draped below the finish cover plate, which is directly above it.

The answer is C.

71.   Which type of brass finish would best prevent tarnish and require the least maintenance?

    A. anodized
    B. organic
    C. oil
    D. wax

Solution

An organic brass finish would best prevent tarnish and require the least maintenance.

Option A is incorrect because anodized finishes are used on aluminum, not brass. Options C and D are incorrect because oil and wax, while limiting tarnish, require more maintenance than do organic coatings.

The answer is B.

72.   Which of the following is not a copper alloy?

    A. austenitic stainless steel
    B. Monel metal
    C. Muntz metal
    D. nickel silver

Solution

Stainless steel is an alloy of iron, carbon, and chromium. Austenitic stainless steel, the most common type, also contains some nickel and/or manganese. This kind of steel is nonmagnetic and not heat treatable.

Monel is a trade name for a metal alloy of copper and nickel. Muntz metal is a common alloy of 60% copper and 40% tin. Nickel silver is a name given to an alloy of 65% copper, 25% zinc, and 10% nickel.

The answer is A.

73. Which of the following additives is NOT added to steel to improve corrosion resistance?

    A. chromium
    B. copper
    C. tungsten
    D. molybdenum

Solution

Chromium, copper, and molybdenum as well as nickel are all used as alloys to improve steel's resistance to corrosion.

Tungsten is added to steel to improve the material's ability to retain its strength when exposed to high temperatures.

The answer is C.

74. Two advantages of using a copper roof are its

I. workability
II. resistance to denting
III. cost
IV. resistance to corrosion

    A. I and II
    B. I and IV
    C. II and III
    D. III and IV

Solution

The advantages of copper roofs include their workability and corrosion resistance, so items I and IV are correct. Copper roofs are expensive and relatively soft (making them susceptible to denting), so items II and III are not advantages of using them.

The answer is B.

75. What percentage of carbon does structural steel typically contain?

    A. above 2.0%
    B. from 0.50% to 0.80%
    C. from 0.20% to 0.50%
    D. from 0.06% to 0.30%

Solution

Steel with over 2.0% carbon is classified as cast iron. The other options are all used, but option C is considered medium-carbon steel and is the most common.

The answer is C.

76. Galvanic action can be avoided by

    A. using neoprene spacers
    B. increasing the thickness of the materials
    C. reducing contact with dripping water
    D. all of the above

Solution

Dissimilar metals should be physically separated by non-conducting materials such as neoprene in order to prevent galvanic action.

Increasing the thickness of the materials may postpone their complete deterioration but will not prevent it, so option B is incorrect. Direct contact with water will speed up galvanic action, but even moisture in the air is sufficient to cause it, so option C is incorrect.

The answer is A.

77. Joining two metals with heat and a filler metal with a melting point above 800°F (427°C) is called

    A. annealing
    B. soldering
    C. brazing
    D. welding

Solution

Welding is joining two metals by heating them above their melting points. *Soldering* is joining two metals using lead-based or tin-based alloys as filler metals that melt below 500°F (260°C).

The answer is C.

78. Which of the following would NOT help to minimize oil canning?

    A. Design attachment hardware that allows panels to move in response to expansion and contraction caused by changes in temperature.
    B. Include information in the specifications that requires the installer to transport panels vertically rather than horizontally.
    C. Specify a high-gloss painted finish on the panels.
    D. Carefully coordinate the design of the supporting structure to ensure that it is level and plumb.

Solution

Oil canning gives a metal siding panel a wavy appearance. Generally, it is not a structural issue, just an aesthetic one. However, it can be minimized through careful design of the panels, attachment hardware, and supporting structure. For example, a textured, ribbed, or matte finish will minimize the appearance of waviness more than a smooth, glossy finish. Allowing space at the hardware connections for expansion and contraction will also help to minimize the waviness.

Most of the things that can be done to minimize oil canning fall under the responsibility of the contractor in the field, but the techniques can be written into the architect's specifications to ensure proper handling of materials and installation. Panels should always be transported vertically rather than horizontally, and care should be taken not to twist them. The supporting structure should be as flat, or planar, as possible.

A good summary of oil canning can be found in the Technical Publications section of the Metal Construction Association website, www.mca1.org. Click on "Technical Resources," then "Publications," and then select "Oil Canning" from the list of technical bulletins. A current link to this article can also be found at **ppi2pass.com/AREresources**.

The answer is C.

WOOD

79. Which of the following defects would most affect a wood joist's ability to resist horizontal shear?

    A. knot
    B. split
    C. wane
    D. warp

Solution

A split is a separation of the wood fibers along the grain that extends through the piece of lumber. Because the value of horizontal shear depends on the integrity of the wood along its grain, any break would reduce the ability of the wood to resist horizontal shear.

Terms to Know

knot: a branch or limb embedded in a tree that is cut through in the process of lumber manufacture

wane: the presence of bark or absence of wood from any cause on the edge or corner of a piece of lumber

warp: any deviation from the plane surface of a piece of lumber

The answer is B.

80. The straightest, most uniform grain appearance in board lumber is achieved by specifying

    A. plain sawing
    B. quarter sawing
    C. rift sawing
    D. rotary sawing

Solution

With the *rift sawing* method, each cut for a board is made by sawing a quarter section of log radially toward the center point of the tree. This requires the quarter section of log being sawn to be shifted slightly for each cut. The grain in the resulting boards is nearly perpendicular to the face of the board. This gives the straightest grain pattern. Rift sawing is normally reserved for oak, to reduce the appearance of flaking, which is caused by medullary cells in the oak.

Quarter sawing is similar to rift sawing except that the quartered log is held in a stationary position as the cuts are made toward the center point of the tree. Yields for this type of sawing are higher than those for rift sawing, but boards made by cutting away from the center will have grains at a slight angle to the face of the board. *Plain sawing* cuts an entire log in one direction. Although plain sawing makes the most efficient use of the tree, boards cut near the tree edges will have a less uniform grain pattern. Rotary sawing is not an accurate term; rotary *slicing* is used only for veneer, not boards.

The answer is C.

81.   Which diagram represents flush overlay cabinet construction?

A.

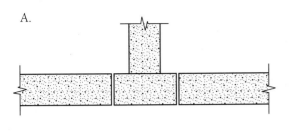

B.

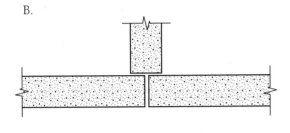

C.

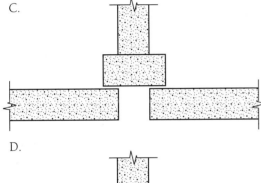

D.

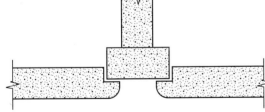

Solution

Flush overlay cabinet construction consists of drawer and door fronts aligned flush with each other with only a slight gap between them. As shown in the diagram, there is generally no face frame.

Option A represents flush construction. Option C represents reveal overlay construction, and option D represents lipped overlay construction.

The answer is B.

82.   In order to get a countertop or cabinet to fit snugly against a slightly irregular partition, which of the following should be specified or called out on the drawings?

    A.   astragal
    B.   extended frame
    C.   scribe
    D.   shoe molding

Solution

A *scribe* is an integral part of woodwork or a separate piece of trim that is cut, sanded, or otherwise shaped on the jobsite to exactly match the irregularities of an adjacent material.

The answer is C.

83.   The detail shown illustrates the

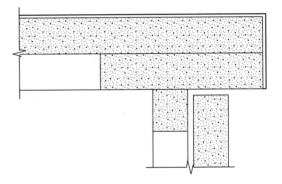

    A.   top of a bookcase
    B.   edge of a cabinet countertop
    C.   front of a closet
    D.   edge of a display cabinet

Solution

The detail shows the built-up top of a countertop, as well as a frame and the top portion of a cabinet door. This would most likely be a countertop edge.

Option A is incorrect because a bookcase would not have the thicker, built-up top or a frame piece and probably would not have a door. Option C is incorrect because the framing for a closet either would be adjacent to a ceiling or would not include the thicker, built-up top piece. Option D is incorrect because a display cabinet would probably not have a door.

The answer is B.

84. Which of the following engineered products would be best to use in place of traditional wood joists for spans from 16 ft (5 m) to 20 ft (6 m)?

- A. wood I-joists
- B. glued-laminated members
- C. medium-density fiberboard
- D. parallel-chord wood trusses

Solution

Wood I-joists are designed to replace standard solid wood joists and rafters and would be very efficient, in terms of both cost and structure, for the spans indicated.

Glued-laminated (glulam) members would be more expensive and heavier than necessary for standard floor or roof framing in these span ranges. Medium-density fiberboard is a panel product and is not designed for structural uses such as beams or joists. Parallel-chord wood trusses could be used, but they are more efficiently used for longer spans.

The answer is A.

85. A lengthwise separation in a piece of rough carpentry that occurs between or through the growth rings is called a

- A. check
- B. shake
- C. split
- D. wane

Solution

A lengthwise separation in a piece of rough carpentry occurring between or through the growth rings is known as a *shake*.

A *check* is a separation of the wood fibers occurring across or through the growth rings. A *split* is similar to a check except that the separation extends completely through the lumber, usually at the ends. A *wane* is the presence of bark or absence of wood, from any cause, on the edge or corner of a piece of lumber.

> *Study Note:* Know the various types of wood defects and the types of warping, including the bow warp, crook warp, and cup warp.

The answer is B.

86. Solid wood members with a nominal thickness between 2 in (51) and 5 in (127) and a nominal width 2 in (51) or greater are called

- A. boards
- B. dimension lumber
- C. timbers
- D. yard lumber

Solution

Solid wood members with a nominal thickness between 2 in (51) and 5 in (127) and a nominal width of 2 in (51) or greater are known as *dimension lumber*.

Boards are pieces of lumber less than 2 in (51) thick and 2 in (51) or more in width. *Timbers* are pieces of lumber 5 in (127) or more in thickness and 5 in (127) or more in width. *Yard lumber* is just a general term for softwood lumber used for structural purposes without regard for specific sizes.

The answer is B.

87. Fire-cut joists are required in

- A. platform framing
- B. heavy timber framing
- C. concrete walls
- D. masonry walls

Solution

A *fire-cut joist* is one with the ends cut at an angle such that the longer end rests on a masonry bearing wall and the shorter end is flush with the inside face of the wall. Fire-cut joists are required in masonry walls to prevent the masonry from being pushed up and out if the wood member should collapse during a fire.

The answer is D.

88. In order to minimize the space required for wood floor framing, the architect would most likely detail the connections to show the use of

- A. hurricane straps
- B. post caps
- C. saddle hangers
- D. splice plates

Solution

Saddle hangers are pieces of preformed metal, designed to fit over a beam, that provide support for joists framed perpendicularly to the beam. This type of connection hardware allows the joists to be installed with their top edges flush with the top edges of the beams. It avoids the requirement that the joists be placed over the beams, which would increase the total depth required for the floor structure.

The answer is C.

89. The horizontal member that holds individual pieces of shoring in place is called a

    A. waler

    B. breast board

    C. raker

    D. none of the above

Solution

Breast boards are horizontal boards between soldier beams, and rakers are diagonal braces that support walers.

The answer is A.

90. A nominal 3 × 6 piece of lumber is classified as

    A. timber

    B. a board

    C. dimension lumber

    D. a yard

Solution

Any piece of lumber from 2 in (51) to 5 in (127) nominal thickness is considered dimension lumber. Timber is lumber 5 in (127) and over, whereas boards are 2 in (51) or less.

The answer is C.

91. Select the INCORRECT statement from among the following.

    A. The larger the pennyweight, the longer the nail.

    B. Design values for bolts are dependent on the thickness of the wood in which they are located.

    C. Split-ring connectors are often used for heavily loaded wood structures that must be disassembled.

    D. In general, lag bolts have more holding power than large screws.

Solution

Shear plates, not split ring connectors, are used for structures that must be disassembled. The face of the shear plate is flush with the face of the lumber, and the two pieces are connected with a bolt.

The answer is C.

92. Which of the following most affects lumber strength?

    A. a split

    B. a wane

    C. a check

    D. a shake

Solution

A split extends completely through the wood, so this would affect both horizontal shear resistance and bending strength. The other defects listed extend only partially into the wood.

The answer is A.

93. Which three of the following are of most importance in wood frame construction?

I. sheathing type

II. differential shrinkage

III. location of defects

IV. firestops

V. headers

    A. I, II, and III

    B. I, II, and IV

    C. II, III, and V

    D. III, IV, and V

Solution

The location of defects is not as important because the characteristics of defects are implied in the grading of the lumber. Headers are not of prime importance.

The answer is B.

94. The allowable stress ratings for lumber in the building codes are based primarily on

    A. size groups
    B. species
    C. types of defects
    D. all of the above

Solution

The allowable stress ratings for lumber in the building codes are based primarily on size groups, species, and types of defects.

The answer is D.

95. Architectural woodwork for installation in the southwestern United States should have a moisture content of

    A. less than 5%
    B. 4% to 9%
    C. 5% to 10%
    D. 8% to 13%

Solution

The southwestern portion of the United States is the driest, so moisture content should approximate the conditions in which the lumber will be used. However, it is difficult to reduce the moisture content much below 5%, so option A is an unrealistic answer.

The answer is B.

96. As a general rule, the length of the three sides of the work triangle in a residential kitchen should not exceed

    A. 20 ft (6.1 m)
    B. 23 ft (7.0 m)
    C. 26 ft (7.9 m)
    D. 30 ft (9.1 m)

Solution

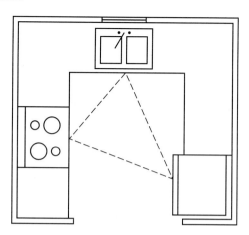

The *work triangle* is an imaginary line drawn from the refrigerator workstation to the sink workstation to the cooking workstation and back again. The three sides of the triangle should add up to no more than 26 ft (7.9 m). A larger work triangle results in an inefficient use of space, and the distances between work areas are too great.

The answer is C.

MOISTURE PROTECTION AND THERMAL INSULATION

97. Which of the following is the best sealant to use between exterior, precast concrete wall panels?

    A. acrylic
    B. butyl
    C. latex
    D. polyurethane

Solution

Polyurethane sealant, either one-part or two-part, provides excellent resistance to weather and is capable of 25% to 50% movement. It can span the wide joints typical of precast concrete, is available in colors, and can be painted.

Acrylics are unsuitable for this situation because of their limited potential for joint movement and their inability to fill the large-width joints that are typical of precast concrete. Butyls are unsuitable because of their limited joint movement and because they are only available in darker colors. They are generally used for areas under water. Latex sealants also have limited joint movement capability and are typically used for joints with no expected movement, such as those around door and window frames.

The answer is D.

98. The minimum suggested pitch for a normal-slope asphalt or composition shingle roof is

    A. 2:12
    B. 3:12
    C. 4:12
    D. 5:12

Solution

A normal-slope asphalt or composition shingle roof should have a minimum pitch of 4:12.

    Study Note: A low-slope asphalt or composition shingle roof can be as low as 2:12, but a double layer of roofing felt is required, and most manufacturers do not recommend this slope. Most questions relating to shingle roofing will probably deal with the standard type of roof.

The answer is C.

99. Many problems associated with exterior insulation and finish systems (EIFS) can be solved using which of the following design techniques?

    A. Design the wall using the rain screen principle.
    B. Use expansion joints at a maximum spacing of 10 ft 0 in (3000).
    C. Increase the thickness of the finish coat.
    D. Provide extra flashing at window and door joints.

Solution

A standard EIFS is designed as a barrier against moisture. The level of moisture prevention depends on the finish and the proper construction of joints and details. An EIFS can experience problems if water leaks behind the finish and insulation and becomes trapped, damaging framing and other building components. Some proprietary systems are available that incorporate the rain screen principle by using a mesh or some other means of allowing pressure to equalize outside and inside of the system. Any water that does leak through is drained to the outside through weep holes.

    Study Note: The other common problem with a standard polymer-based (PB) EIFS is puncturing or denting. This can be addressed by using a polymer-modified system (PM) or by using a high-impact PB system with fiberglass mesh and an extra layer of base coat.

The answer is A.

100. Which of the following materials provides the highest insulation value (*R*-value)?

    A. expanded perlite
    B. expanded polystyrene
    C. fiberglass
    D. polyisocyanurate

Solution

Polyisocyanurate has the highest *R*-value. For a 1 in thickness, its *R*-value ranges from 6.25 ft²-hr-°F/Btu to 7.20 ft²-hr-°F/Btu (43.8 m²·K/W to 51.8 m²·K/W). Polystyrene has the next highest value, at 5.00 ft²-hr-°F/Btu (34.7 m²·K/W).

The answer is D.

101. A vapor barrier placed on the exterior side of the insulation in a wall would be MOST appropriate in a

    A. cold climate
    B. temperate climate
    C. hot, humid climate
    D. hot, dry climate

Solution

Vapor barriers should be placed on the "warm" side of insulation, to prevent water vapor from condensing to liquid water when its temperature drops below the dew point. In cold or temperate climates, the warm side of the insulation is toward the inside of the building. However, in hot, humid climates, the warmer, moister outside air vapor can condense when it reaches the cooler, air-conditioned interior of the building, which is why the vapor barrier is placed on the exterior side of the insulation in this case.

The answer is C.

102. The sketch shown is of a wall in a cold climate. Where should the vapor barrier be located?

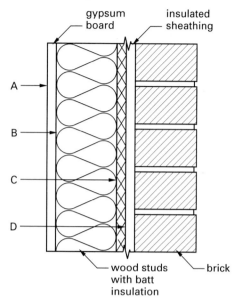

Solution

Vapor barriers should always be located on the warm side of insulation (area B) to prevent moisture from condensing when it cools and reaches the dew point. Moisture penetrating the insulation can reduce the insulation's effectiveness and damage other materials.

The answer is B.

103. Asphalt-impregnated building paper is used under siding primarily to

    A. improve thermal resistance
    B. increase the water resistance of the wall
    C. act as a vapor barrier
    D. all of the above

Solution

Although asphalt-impregnated paper can act as a vapor barrier, the fact that it is placed on the outside of the sheathing precludes options C and D from being correct. It does add a little to the thermal resistance, but its primary purpose is to prevent any water that seeps behind the siding from getting into the structure. It also serves to prevent air infiltration.

The answer is B.

104. Which of the following would be LEAST appropriate for insulating a steel stud wall?

    A. polystyrene boards
    B. rock wool
    C. fiberglass batts
    D. perlite boards

Solution

Rock wool is a loose insulation poured or blown into cavities. It is usually not used in commercial construction and can settle when installed in any type of cavity wall. The other types of insulation listed would be more appropriate, although fiberglass batts would be difficult because the usual method of attaching them is stapling the flanges of the insulation to wood studs. However, fiberglass batts could be fit in steel stud cavities by friction.

The answer is B.

105. Which of the following would be most appropriate for dampproofing an above-grade concrete wall with a moderately rough surface?

    A. cementitious coating
    B. bituminous coating
    C. synthetic rubber
    D. silicone coating

Solution

Silicone coatings would provide the best coverage for rough walls because they can be sprayed, painted, or rolled on. If the wall was below grade, the correct choice would be a cementitious coating or a bituminous coating.

The answer is D.

106. What is used to keep water from penetrating an expansion joint at the intersection of a roof and wall?

    A. base flashing
    B. counterflashing
    C. sealant
    D. coping

Solution

Base flashing extends from the roof over the cant strip and up the wall, so option A is incorrect. Counter flashing covers the base flashing to extend from the wall over the base flashing and to cover any expansion joint that may occur at this point. Coping protects the top of the parapet, so option D is incorrect. Sealants by themselves are not adequate to cover a major expansion joint as would occur at the roof and wall intersection, so option C is incorrect.

The answer is B.

107. Which material has the lowest perm rating?

    A. 10 mil (0.25) polyethylene
    B. gypsum wallboard
    C. 1 mil (0.025) aluminum foil
    D. exterior oil paint

Solution

Perm rating is a measurement of how much moisture passes through a certain material in a given amount of time. ASTM E96 defines it as "the passage of one grain of water vapor per hour through one square foot of a material at a pressure differential of 1 in of mercury." (In SI units, the definition is "one nanogram per second per square meter per pascal of pressure.")

Vapor retarders are selected based on their perm ratings. The best vapor retarders have the lowest ratings. This problem is essentially asking which of the listed materials is the best vapor retarder, and the answer is option C, aluminum foil, with a perm rating of zero. Polyethylene is the next best, with a perm rating of 0.03 (0.0005). Three coats of exterior oil paint have a perm rating of 1.6 to 3.0 (0.028 to 0.052). Gypsum wallboard allows the most moisture to pass through, with a perm rating of 50.

The answer is C.

DOORS, WINDOWS, AND GLAZING

108. The dimension labeled x in the diagram refers to a

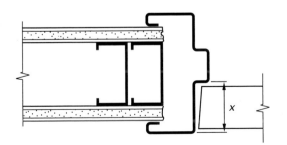

    A. face
    B. rabbet
    C. soffit
    D. stop

Solution

The space in which the door closes in a door frame is called the *rabbet*.

The *face* is the portion of the frame parallel to the wall. The *soffit* is the width of the frame portion serving as the stop. The *stop* is the portion against which the door shuts.

    Study Note: Know the basic terminology of all types of construction components.

The answer is B.

109. In wood door frame construction, the function of the shim is to

    A. provide the required space for hardware
    B. prevent sound from leaking through the opening
    C. hide the gap between the frame and partition
    D. provide for adjustability in setting the frame plumb

Solution

A *shim* is a tapered piece of wood that, when used in pairs, allows the position of a door frame to be adjusted along the door's height until the frame is plumb.

The answer is D.

110. A slip joint is used in the head of an aluminum storefront system to

    A. allow for expansion and contraction
    B. accommodate the deflection of the structure
    C. facilitate the installation of the mullions
    D. provide a way to install and remove the glazing

Solution

Any deflection of the structure above a storefront could possibly break the glass or bend the mullions. A slip joint is used to prevent the weight of the structure above from bearing on the framing or the glazing.

The answer is B.

111. Which of the windows illustrated would be best for ventilation during heavy rainstorms?

A.

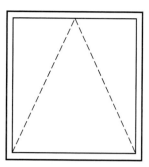

B.

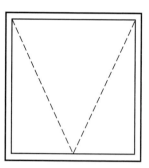

C.

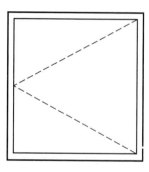

D.

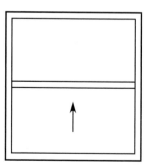

Solution

Option A represents an awning window that pivots on the top. As such, the window could be left open during a rainstorm and still keep water out of the building. All three of the incorrect choices would allow water to enter more easily.

Option B shows a hopper window. Option C illustrates a casement window, and option D illustrates a single-hung window.

The answer is A.

112. Which of the following types of glass is the strongest?

    A. laminated
    B. annealed
    C. tempered
    D. heat-strengthened

Solution

Laminated glass is the strongest of the four types of glass listed. It consists of two or more layers of glass with a layer of plastic bonded in between. If the glazing is broken, the pieces of glass will be held together by the layer of plastic. Laminated glass is used in applications such as bulletproof glazing, car windshields, and skylights.

Annealed glass, or ordinary window glass, is made by floating molten glass on top of molten tin. As the liquid moves through the production process, it is slowly cooled into a perfectly flat sheet of solid glass. Annealed glass may be subjected to processes such as tempering and heat strengthening to change its characteristics.

Tempered and *heat-strengthened* glass are both formed by heating annealed glass to very high temperatures. Heat-strengthened glass is heated and then cooled slowly. Tempered glass is heated to higher temperatures and then cooled quickly. Tempered glass is about twice as strong as heat-strengthened glass and about four times as strong as annealed glass. Tempered glass is used in glass doors and windows, as shelving, and for many other uses where a safety glass is required.

The answer is A.

113. Tempered glass is required in

    A. entry doors
    B. sidelights with sills below 18 in (457)
    C. glazing within 1 ft (305) of doors
    D. all of the above

Solution

Safety glazing is required in all areas subject to human impact. This includes glass doors and any glass within 24 in (610) of doors. Glass farther than 24 in (610) from doors and with a sill over 18 in (457) above the floor does not have to be safety glazed.

The answer is D.

114. What type of glass would probably NOT be appropriate for a 10-story building?

    A. tempered
    B. annealed
    C. heat-strengthened
    D. laminated

Solution

Annealed glass is the standard glass used in most noncritical glazing situations. All of the other types of glass listed have greater strengths and could be used in a tall building with large panels of glass subject to high wind loads and thermal cycling.

The answer is B.

115. Select the INCORRECT statement concerning fire-rated door assemblies.

    A. Hinges must always be the ball-bearing type.
    B. Under some circumstances a closer is not needed.
    C. Labeling is required for both the door and frame.
    D. The maximum width is 4 ft 0 in (1220).

Solution

Closers are always required for fire-rated doors. The other statements are correct.

The answer is B.

116. Which of the sketches depicts a half surface hinge?

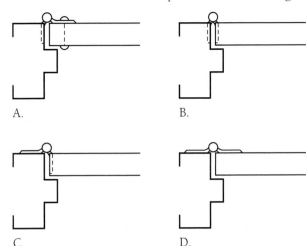

A.   B.

C.   D.

Solution

Option A depicts a half surface hinge. Option B depicts a full mortise hinge, option C a half mortise hinge, and option D a full surface hinge.

The answer is A.

117. In what part of a panel door is the lockset mounted?

    A. stile
    B. mullion
    C. keyway
    D. rail

Solution

The lockset of a panel door is mounted in the stile.

The answer is A.

118. Which type of lock would be most appropriate for an entry door into an office suite?

    A. cylindrical lock
    B. unit lock
    C. mortise lock
    D. rim lock

Solution

A mortise lock offers the most flexibility in the number of operating functions available and is a very durable type of lockset. The next best choice would be a cylindrical lock.

The answer is C.

119. Which of the following windows could be used as an emergency escape and rescue opening?

A.

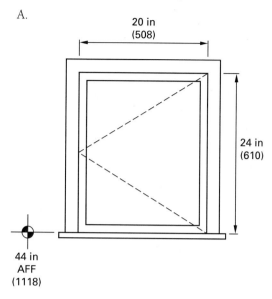

C.

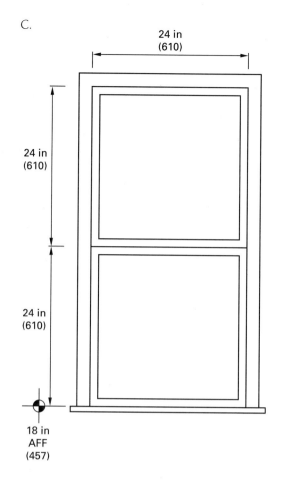

B.

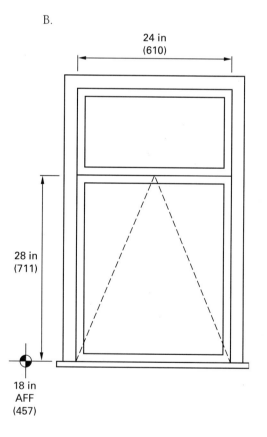

D.

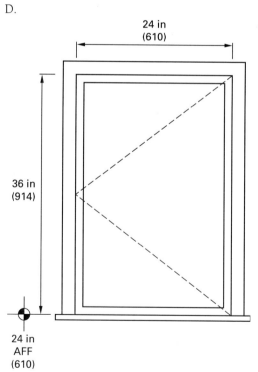

Solution

Emergency escape and rescue openings (sometimes referred to as *egress windows*) must be provided in all sleeping areas in residential occupancies. They provide a way for inhabitants to escape or for a firefighter to enter. Requirements vary for sleeping areas in nonresidential applications, such as dormitories and hotels; consult the applicable code in that jurisdiction.

All the following requirements must be satisfied for a window to qualify as an emergency escape and rescue window, according to the *International Residential Code* and the *International Building Code*.

- minimum width of opening: 20 in (508)

- minimum height of opening: 24 in (610)

- minimum net clear opening: 5.0 ft^2 (1.5 m^2) ground floor, 5.7 ft^2 (1.7 m^2) upper floors

- maximum sill height: 44 in (1118)

Awning windows are not acceptable for use as emergency escape and rescue openings. If a double-hung window is used, the bottom pane must satisfy the dimensional and area requirements when open. Casement windows are a good choice, but again, the dimensional and area requirements must be satisfied. The window in option D satisfies the requirements with a width of 24 in (610), a height of 36 in (914), and a net clear opening of 6 ft^2 (1.8 m^2). In addition, the sill height is within the required range at less than 44 in (1118) above the finish floor. Each of the other three windows has less than 5 ft^2 (1.5 m^2) of net clear opening.

The answer is D.

120. Which of these statements are FALSE?

I. A fire rating of 1½ hours is the maximum possible for a steel door.

II. The frames for a steel door are normally 12-, 14-, or 16-gage, depending on use.

III. Steel doors must be used with steel frames.

IV. Hinges or offset pivots can be used with steel doors.

V. The standard thickness of a steel door is 1³/₈ in (35).

    A. I and V only

    B. II and IV only

    C. I, III, and V only

    D. II, III, and V only

Solution

Statement I is incorrect because ratings up to 3 hours are possible. Statement V is incorrect because the standard thickness is 1³/₄ in (44).

The answer is A.

121. In the window elevation shown, what is indicated by label *x*?

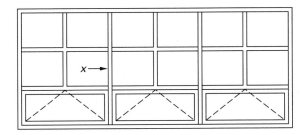

    A. mullion

    B. muntin

    C. stile

    D. rail

Solution

Mullions are members that separate large sections of glass, whereas *muntins* are the framing that separates individual panes of glass. *Stiles* are vertical members of doors, and *rails* are horizontal members of doors.

The answer is A.

122. The pieces that make up an aluminum window are most often formed by

    A. rolling

    B. extruding

    C. drawing

    D. casting

Solution

Most pieces of aluminum door and window frames are made through a process called *extrusion*. The metal is pushed through a die to form the desired shape. For assemblies that are produced multiple times and with pieces with the same profiles (such as windows), extrusion is a very economical process. *Drawing* is similar to extrusion but the metal is pulled rather than pushed through the die.

Steel is often formed through *rolling*. The metal travels through a series of rollers and is formed into the proper shape. Metal can either be *hot rolled* or *cold rolled*. Hot rolling eliminates flaws, and cold rolling increases strength.

Casting is the process of pouring molten metal into a form and allowing it to harden.

The answer is B.

FINISH MATERIALS

123. A gypsum wallboard ceiling detail is shown.

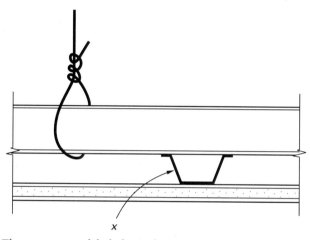

The component labeled *x* is the

    A. channel spacer
    B. cold-rolled steel channel
    C. furring channel
    D. main runner

Solution

The illustration shows a standard method of installing gypsum wallboard ceilings. The components shown include the gypsum wallboard attached to the furring channel. Furring channels are normally installed 24 in (600) on center and are attached to 1¹/₂ in (38) cold-rolled steel channels placed 48 in (1200) on center. The cold-rolled steel channels are suspended from the structure above with wire.

The answer is C.

124. Which of the following types of wood floors would be the LEAST appropriate for a commercial office?

    A. block
    B. parquet
    C. resilient
    D. strip

Solution

Resilient wood floors are commonly used for theater stages, dance floors, and gymnasiums. They provide extra bounce and resiliency for these types of uses.

The answer is C.

125. Which of the following flooring types has the highest resilience?

    A. asphalt
    B. cork
    C. linoleum
    D. vinyl composition

Solution

Cork is a very resilient material. Its resilience is similar to that of rubber tile.

Asphalt tile, which is seldom used, has the lowest resilience. Linoleum and vinyl composition tile have low to moderate resilience.

The answer is B.

126. The standardized levels of finish in the gypsum wallboard industry refer, among other things, to the

    A. quality of workmanship of the final finish
    B. number of coats of joint compound used
    C. thickness of joint compound used
    D. type of texturing used

Solution

The Gypsum Association publishes *Recommended Levels of Gypsum Board Finish*, which gives six levels of finish. One requirement for these levels is the number of coats of joint compound used. The levels are 0, 1, 2, 3, 4, and 5. Level 0 requires no taping, finish, or accessories, while Level 5 requires three coats of joint compound over joints and fastener heads, as well as a final skim coat over the entire surface of the wall.

The answer is B.

127. Which paint type would serve best as an anti-graffiti coating?

    A. acrylic
    B. alkyd
    C. oil
    D. urethane

Solution

Urethane is a high-performance coating and has superior resistance to abrasion, grease, alcohol, water, and fuels. It resists the adhesion of graffiti to surfaces and allows relatively easy removal of graffiti.

    Study Note: Problems on paints and coatings are common on the ARE. Review the various types of paints and their qualities, uses, and formulations.

The answer is D.

128. In order to achieve the most uniform, straight-grain appearance in wood paneling, which of the following should be specified?

    A. plain slicing
    B. rotary slicing
    C. quarter slicing
    D. half-round slicing

Solution

Plain slicing produces a figured pattern with a characteristic "cathedral" appearance. Rotary slicing produces the most varied grain pattern, and half-round slicing yields a moderate amount of pattern. Because quarter slicing cuts perpendicular to the growth rings, this gives the straightest pattern of the choices listed. Rift slicing would also give a very uniform grain pattern.

The answer is C.

129. The portion of paint that evaporates or dries is called the

    A. binder
    B. pigment
    C. solvent
    D. vehicle

Solution

The vehicle consists of two parts: the nonvolatile part called the *binder*, which forms the final coating, and the volatile part called the *solvent*, which evaporates or dries. Pigments, if added, are part of the vehicle and form the color of the coating.

The answer is C.

130. In determining the width and gage of gypsum board framing, what are some of the important considerations?

  I.   thickness of the gypsum board
  II. spacing of studs
  III. height of the wall
  IV. size of piping and other built-in items
  V. number of layers to be supported

    A. I, II, and V only
    B. I, III, IV, and V only
    C. II, III, and IV only
    D. II, III, IV, and V only

Solution

The thickness of the gypsum board is not critical because there is little difference in the weights of $^3/_8$, $^1/_2$, and $^5/_8$ in (10, 13, and 16) boards. The number of layers, on the other hand, can affect the total weight significantly.

The answer is D.

131. Which of the following statements about veneer stone is FALSE?

    A. It can be fabricated $^3/_8$ in (10) thick.
    B. Copper or steel clamps are used to anchor the stone to the substrate.
    C. Only special types of portland cement mortar or sealants should be used in the joints.
    D. It can be supported on masonry, concrete, steel, or wood framing.

Solution

Only noncorrosive metals, such as stainless steel, should be used to anchor stone. Both copper and steel would deteriorate over time.

The answer is B.

132. Which of the following is the most important consideration in detailing a wood-strip floor?

    A. flame-spread rating
    B. expansion space at the perimeter
    C. nailing method
    D. moisture protection from below

Solution

All of the choices listed are considerations in detailing wood floors, so select the *most* important. Moisture is one of the biggest problems with wood floors, and keeping moisture out in the first place would minimize other problems such as expansion at the perimeter. Therefore, option D is the best choice.

The answer is D.

133. Ceramic mosaic tile in a public shower room is best installed over

    A. water-resistant gypsum board
    B. a bed of portland cement mortar
    C. concrete block walls coated with a waterproofing membrane
    D. rigid cement composition board made for this purpose

Solution

A full bed of portland cement mortar offers the best durability and water resistance for high-use, wet areas.

The answer is B.

134. On floors subject to deflection, both terrazzo and granite installations should include

    A. a membrane
    B. a latex additive in the mortar
    C. thinset mortar
    D. a sand cushion

Solution

A membrane is part of a total assembly that also includes reinforcing and a thick bed of mortar on which the granite is laid or that is part of the terrazzo. The membrane allows the structural slab to move independently of the finish flooring so that any deflection does not crack the floor.

The answer is A.

135. An architect is writing specifications for a small clothing boutique. The architect has worked closely with the talented owner and fashion designer to plan an intricately detailed tile floor for the main showroom. The designer wishes to use a type of marble she saw installed in a friend's home in Rome. Which type of tile specification is most appropriate?

    A. prescriptive
    B. proprietary
    C. descriptive
    D. reference standard

Solution

A *proprietary* specification would be appropriate in this situation because it would give the architect the most control over the product provided and installed by the contractor. The architect and owner would have the opportunity to select the products they want to use for the floor and would refer to those specific products in the specification. A proprietary specification is a type of closed, or *prescriptive*, specification.

Descriptive and *reference standard* specifications are types of open specifications. They outline the final results desired but do not specifically tell the contractor what materials to use. Descriptive specifications require the architect to list all of the desired characteristics of the material and put the onus on the contractor to find a product that will satisfy the requirements. They can be difficult to write because of the level of detail that must be included to ensure that an appropriate product is chosen. A reference standard specification is much simpler to write. It refers to industry standards to define the desired characteristics of materials and installation systems.

The answer is B.

136. Materials or assemblies with a high NRC generally have a

    A. high STC
    B. low STC
    C. high reverberation time
    D. low absorption coefficient

Solution

Materials or assemblies with a high NRC generally have a low STC. The NRC, or *noise reduction coefficient*, is a measure of how absorptive a material is to sound. Materials with a high NRC are generally very porous materials such as acoustical ceiling tile, fabrics, carpet, and so on. The STC, or *sound transmission coefficient*, measures how well a material blocks sound transmission from one space to the next.

The *absorption coefficient* is linked to the NRC, but they are directly proportional; high NRCs equal high absorption coefficients. *Reverberation time* is a calculation for a space rather than a property of a material or assembly.

The answer is B.

137. A tactile finish should be applied to hardware on a door that leads to a building's

    A. fire stairs
    B. boiler room
    C. restrooms
    D. exterior

Solution

A tactile finish (rough surface) is applied to hardware on doors leading to building areas that would be dangerous for a person with impaired vision, such as a boiler room.

The answer is B.

VERTICAL TRANSPORTATION

138. Which of the following types of elevators is used for high-rise office buildings?

    A. standard hydraulic
    B. high-speed hydraulic
    C. geared traction
    D. gearless traction

Solution

Gearless traction is one type of mechanism used for high-speed elevators, which a high-rise building would require.

Geared traction elevators are used for low speed and high capacity. Hydraulic elevators are not appropriate for high-rise buildings; they are used for buildings from two to five stories, or up to about 50 ft (15 m).

The answer is D.

139. For a three-story department store, the most important variable for selecting an elevator would be its

    A. speed
    B. capacity
    C. control method
    D. machine room location

Solution

A department store requires elevators with high capacity. That is, the amount of weight the elevators can carry, which translates into the allowable number of people on the elevator at any one time, is a priority.

For a three-story building, speed is not critical, and the control method and machine room location would be secondary considerations.

> *Study Note:* Understand the different elevator control methods available. These include the single automatic, selective collective, and group automatic. A *single automatic system* answers only one call at a time, and the user has exclusive control of the car until the trip is complete. With a *selective collective system*, the elevator answers all calls in one direction and then reverses direction and answers all calls in the opposite direction. With a *group automatic system*, a computer controls two or more elevators and dispatches and operates all the elevators in the most efficient manner possible.

The answer is B.

140. An underground transit station is best served with

    A. escalators and elevators
    B. stairs and escalators
    C. stairs and elevators
    D. moving walks and elevators

Solution

A transit station must move large numbers of people quickly as well as provide accessibility. A combination of escalators and elevators is the only listed option that meets these requirements.

Stairs may be provided as a secondary method of vertical transportation but would require more room to move the same numbers of people. Moving walks are limited by their maximum slope and speed and would not be appropriate for a transit station.

The answer is A.

141. Which of the following is NOT a standard nominal width for an escalator?

    A. 32 in (800)
    B. 40 in (1000)
    C. 48 in (1200)
    D. 54 in (1400)

Solution

54 in (1400) is not a standard nominal width for an escalator.

Most manufacturers make escalators in nominal widths of 32 in, 40 in, and 48 in (800, 1000, and 1200) with corresponding actual widths of 24 in, 32 in, and 40 in (600, 800, and 1000).

The answer is D.

Problems 142 and 143 refer to the following sketch.

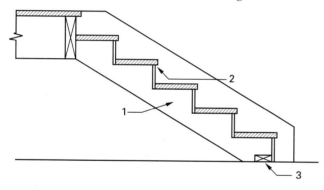

142. The purpose of the block shown at area 3 is to

    A. counteract the thrust of the stair
    B. provide a nailing base for the riser board
    C. give lateral stability to the vertical supports
    D. help locate and lay out the stair

Solution

The block shown at area 3 is used to counteract the thrust of the stair. If this block is not used, the carriages must be toenailed to the floor, which is a weaker construction detail than that shown.

The answer is A.

143. Which of the following are the parts identified by areas 1 and 2, respectively?

  I. tread
  II. nosing
  III. carriage
  IV. ledger
  V. stringer

    A. I and III
    B. II and III
    C. IV and V
    D. V and I

Solution

The member supporting the treads (area 1) is the carriage. The overhanging portion of the tread member (area 2) is the nosing.

The answer is B.

144. The depth of an elevator lobby serving four or more cars should generally not be less than

    A. 6 ft (1800)
    B. $1^{1}/_{2}$ times the depth of the car
    C. 10 ft (3000)
    D. 3 times the depth of the car

Solution

The depth should be at least $1^{1}/_{2}$ times the depth of the car, but no less than 10 ft (3000). Because the question does not give any information about car depth, assume that the minimum depth is the correct answer.

The answer is C.

145. A geared traction elevator would be most appropriate for

    A. a 5-story medical office building
    B. a 16-story office building
    C. a 4-story department store
    D. an 8-story apartment building

Solution

Geared traction elevators can be designed to serve a wide variety of slower speeds and high capacities, so they are ideal for low-rise buildings with heavy loads, such as department stores. A geared traction elevator could be used for a small medical office building, but a higher speed would offer better service. A 16-story office building would need a high-speed, moderate-capacity elevator, so a geared traction type would be inappropriate. An apartment building would require a low capacity but higher speeds.

The answer is C.

146. A reasonable elevator capacity for a medium-sized office building is

    A. 2000 lbm (1000 kg)
    B. 3000 lbm (1500 kg)
    C. 4000 lbm (2000 kg)
    D. 6000 lbm (3000 kg)

Solution

2000 lbm (1000 kg) elevators are only used for small apartments, and 6000 lbm (3000 kg) elevators are used for freight. A 4000 lbm (2000 kg) capacity is often used for large office buildings and retail stores, but 3000 lbm (1500 kg) is more common for small and medium-sized buildings.

The answer is B.

OTHER AREAS

147. Dock levelers are used to

    A. provide final adjustment for steel angle trim
    B. keep boating piers stable in the water
    C. provide adjustability for various sized trucks
    D. accommodate tolerances in pouring concrete pits

Solution

Dock levelers are pieces of equipment used to allow trucks with various bed heights to be serviced from the same dock. The equipment is placed in a pit at the edge of the dock, and a steel panel is adjusted up or down to provide a ramp from the dock to the level of the truck.

The answer is C.

148. Which of the following is NOT required for an access floor system?

    A. lifting devices
    B. modular panels
    C. pedestals
    D. stringers

Solution

Access floor systems may use stringers, which are rigid connections between pedestals, but they can also be the stringerless type, which rely only on pedestals and panels to keep the system in place.

All access floors use modular panels set on pedestals of some type. Removal of the panels requires a lifting device.

The answer is D.

149. Materials for toilet compartments include all of the following EXCEPT

    A. glass-reinforced gypsum
    B. solid polymer
    C. stainless steel
    D. stone

Solution

Glass-reinforced gypsum panels are not available or used for toilet partitions.

Common materials used for toilet compartments include stainless or painted steel, plastic laminate over particleboard, marble or granite, phenolic-core units, and solid polymer fabricated from high-density polyethylene or polypropylene.

The answer is A.

150. Which of the following fire extinguishing agents is being phased out?

    A. carbon dioxide
    B. Halon
    C. nitrogen
    D. wet chemical

Solution

The gas Halon is a very effective fire-extinguishing agent and was once commonly used in computer rooms to put out fires without damaging electrical equipment. Because of environmental concerns regarding ozone depletion, production of Halon ceased in the United States on January 1, 1994. Existing installations are being phased out and replaced with other agents. These include inert gases, such as nitrogen and argon, and various blends of gases.

The answer is B.

151. Which of the following statements are true about built-up roofing?

I.   It is a good choice for flat roofs.
II.   It is best applied only over nailable decks.
III. The top layer should be protected from ultraviolet degradation.
IV.   Proper installation is more important than the number of plies.
V.   Roof insulation can be placed either above or below the roofing.

    A. I, III, and V only
    B. II, III, and IV only
    C. III, IV, and V only
    D. I, II, IV, and V only

Solution

Statement I is incorrect because, although built-up roofs can be applied to flat roofs, they should not be; there should be a minimum of $1/4$ in/ft (20 mm/m) of slope. Statement II is incorrect because built-up roofs can be applied over nailable and non-nailable decks.

The answer is C.

152. An architect in Richmond, Virginia, has been asked to design a replacement roof for a hospital. The existing roof has a slope of approximately 1:12. The building supervisor requests a system that allows for additional insulation to be installed and includes paths of pavers for easy access to mechanical units and other equipment located on the roof. Which type of single-ply roofing system should be recommended?

    A. fully adhered EPDM
    B. loose-laid EPDM
    C. fully adhered PVC
    D. mechanically attached PVC

Solution

A loose-laid, single-ply EPDM roofing system would be a reasonable choice in this situation. The summers in Richmond are hot while the winters can be cold, and EPDM (ethylene propylene diene monomer) rubber weathers extreme temperature fluctuations well. The existing roofing material should be removed down to the roof deck to allow new insulation board to be installed. The EPDM will be installed over the insulation board and topped with a layer of roof pavers or a combination of pavers and ballast.

The answer is B.

153. Which of the following will effectively reduce the possibility of termite infestation?

I.   Design the slope of the grade near the foundation to fall away from the structure.
II.   Specify pressure-treated lumber.
III. Require that soil poison be applied to the footprint area of the building before construction operations begin.
IV.   Provide a gravel drainage area where the foundation wall meets the surrounding grade.

    A. I and III only
    B. II and III only
    C. II and IV only
    D. I, III, and IV only

Solution

There is no way to completely prevent termites from entering a structure, but there are many elements that architects can include in their designs to make the environment less hospitable to insects and, therefore, less prone to the damage they can cause.

Termites, along with many other damaging insects such as carpenter ants, bees, and powderpost beetles, flourish in moisture and wood, and they generally enter buildings at the ground level. (Other types of wood-destroying insects are found in different parts of the country and favor varying environments, so it is important to research the most common types of infestation and design an insect control plan accordingly.) Preventing wooden parts of the structure from coming in contact with the ground is one of the keys. Foundations should also be kept as dry as possible; designing the grade to fall away from the building will help to keep the area well drained. It is important to specify that an appropriate soil poison be applied to the area of the building footprint before construction begins. The type of insecticide used varies depending on the type of insect it is to combat.

Pressure-treating lumber makes the wood more resistant to damage from water but does not make it more resistant to insect damage.

One of the most common errors building owners make is to pile mulch around the base of shrubbery planted at the perimeter of the building. The mulch, whether made of pine bark, cocoa bean shells, gravel, or any other material, holds in the moisture, which is good for plants but bad for the structure. Termites thrive in the warm, moist soil underneath the gravel and can use that as an access point to enter the basement or crawlspace. Using a gravel drainage area in lieu of gutters and downspouts can have the same consequences if the system is not designed to carry the water away from the perimeter of the building.

The answer is A.

154. Which of the following materials would NOT be used as a firestop?

     A. mortar
     B. mineral wool
     C. silicone foam
     D. treated wood blocking

Solution

Firestops are materials or systems of materials that are used to seal penetrations through fire walls or smoke barriers. They are always noncombustible and may be factory built or constructed in the field. Depending on the wall type and application, mortar, mineral wool, or silicone foam would be acceptable for use as a firestop.

Draftstops also prevent the passage of fire and smoke but can be made of combustible materials such as treated wood blocking. They are placed between floors and at concealed spaces.

The answer is D.

155. The Davis-Bacon Act requires that all

     A. U.S. government projects in excess of $2000 be bid
     B. workers on U.S. government projects over $2000 be paid at prevailing wage rates
     C. bids for U.S. government projects be solicited from minority- or women-owned businesses
     D. U.S. government projects be publicly advertised prior to bidding

Solution

The Davis-Bacon Act, enacted in 1931, requires that on projects over $2000 to which the United States or the District of Columbia is a party, all workers will be paid prevailing wage rates. The rates are determined by the secretary of labor in comparison to wage rates for similar classes of workers on similar projects in the area where the work is being performed. The act also requires workers to be paid at least once a week, and allows the government to withhold payments to the contractor, if necessary, so that workers can be paid. If a contractor does not follow the requirements of the act, the act allows the government the option to withhold contracts from that company for three years. Later amendments also require comparable overtime pay and benefits.

Labor costs on projects governed by the Davis-Bacon Act can be considerably higher than similar private-sector projects, and cost opinions should be adjusted accordingly.

The answer is B.

ACCESSIBILITY/RAMP VIGNETTE

Directions

Develop a stair and ramp system and doorway to connect the lower level of an entry lobby to a slightly raised portion of a building as shown on the accompanying floor plan. Indicate all ramps, stairs, railings, walls, doors, and landings required to complete the plan in conformance to the program and code requirements and to principles of design logic. Assume that one 36 in (915) door is required from the exit corridor.

Program

1. Provide an accessible circulation system, including a ramp and stairway, to connect the lower level of the lobby with the exit corridor level.

2. Locate a wall and door on the upper level to separate the lobby from the exit corridor.

3. No portion of the ramp or stairs may encroach on the existing upper level.

4. Show the elevations of all new landings.

Code Requirements

General

1. The minimum width of an exit route shall not be less than 44 in (1120).

2. Projections into a required exit route width are prohibited, except for handrail projections.

3. The space required for a wheelchair to make a 180° turn is a clear space of 60 in (1525) diameter.

Stairs

1. The minimum width shall not be less than 44 in (1120).

2. Projections into a required stairway are prohibited, except for handrail projections.

3. The minimum dimension measured in the direction of travel shall not be less than the width of the stairway.

4. On any given flight of stairs, all steps shall have uniform riser heights and uniform tread widths. Stair treads shall be no less than 11 in (280) wide, measured from riser to riser. Stair risers shall be no more than 7 in (180) and no less than 4 in (100).

Ramps

Any part of an accessible route with a slope greater than 1:20 shall be considered a ramp and shall comply with the three following requirements.

1. The maximum slope of a ramp in new construction shall be 1:12. The maximum rise for any run shall be 30 in (760).

2. The minimum clear width of a ramp shall be 44 in (915). Projections into a required ramp width are prohibited, except for handrail projections.

3. Ramps shall have level landings at the bottom and top of each ramp run, at all points of turning, and at doors. Landings shall have the following features.

   - The landing shall be at least as wide as the ramp run leading to it.

   - The minimum dimension in the direction of travel shall be 60 in (1525).

   - If ramps change direction at landings, the minimum dimension shall be 60 in (1525).

   - If a doorway is located at a landing, the area in front of the doorway shall have maneuvering clearances as described in the code section on doors.

Handrails

1. Stairways and ramps shall have handrails on both sides. Exception: Handrails are not required on ramps where the vertical rise between landings is 6 in (150) or less.

2. Handrails shall be continuous within the full length of each ramp run and stair flight. The inside handrail on switchback and dogleg stairs and ramps shall be continuous.

3. If ramp handrails are not continuous, they shall extend at least 12 in (305) beyond the top and bottom of the ramp segment and shall be parallel with the floor or ground surface.

4. If stair handrails are not continuous, they shall extend at least 12 in (305) beyond the top and bottom risers.

5. Stairways more than 88 in (2235) wide shall have intermediate handrails.

Guardrails

Open sides of landings, floor surfaces, ramps, and stairways shall be protected by a continuous guardrail.

Doors

1. Doorways shall have a minimum clear opening of 32 in (815) with the door open 90°, measured between the face of the door and the opposite stop.

2. Exit doors shall swing in the direction of egress travel.

3. Minimum maneuvering clearances at doors shall be as shown in the following illustration.

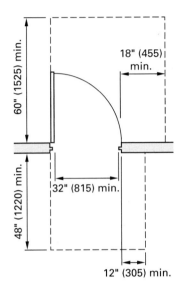

maneuvering clearances at doors

Tips

• Before drawing stairs, calculate how many risers are needed.

• When drawing treads, be careful to make sure the minimum depth is indicated. On the actual exam, the tread depth will be automatically calculated. The tread measurement is displayed in the element information area at the bottom of the work screen.

• Check for overlaps while working by using the check icon on the screen.

• If one element of two overlapping elements cannot be selected, keep clicking without moving the mouse until the desired element is highlighted.

Warnings

• Be sure to understand the existing elevations and indicate the new elevations of all landings.

Tools

Useful tools include the following.

• *zoom* tool for checking clearances and overlapping elements

• *sketch circle* tool to indicate required handrail extensions and door maneuvering clearances

• full-screen cursor to help line up elements

Target Time: 45 minutes

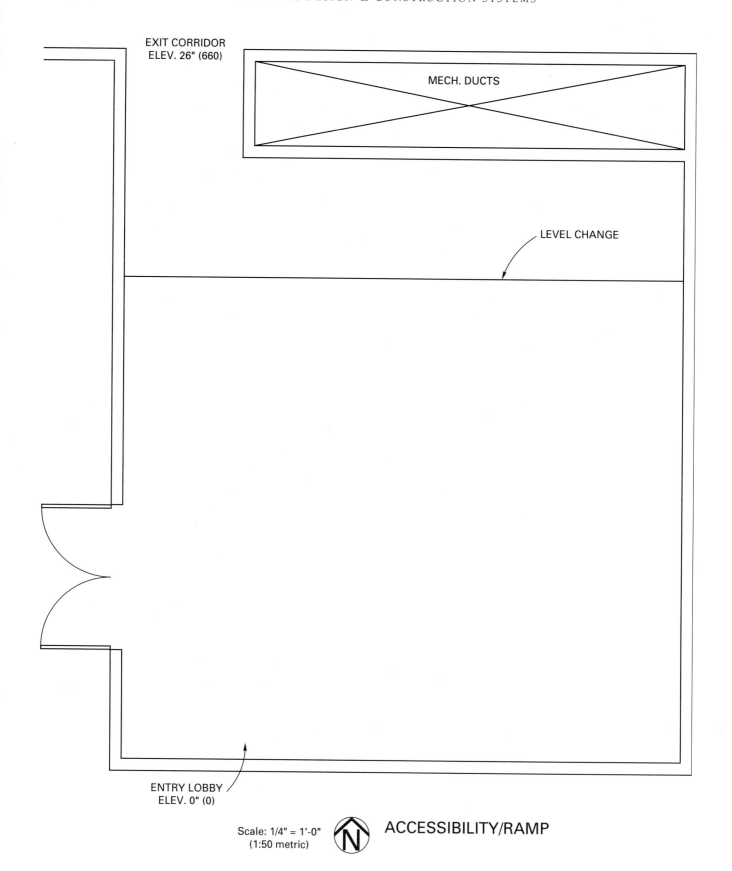

EXIT CORRIDOR
ELEV. 26" (660)

MECH. DUCTS

LEVEL CHANGE

ENTRY LOBBY
ELEV. 0" (0)

Scale: 1/4" = 1'-0"   ACCESSIBILITY/RAMP
(1:50 metric)

ACCESSIBILITY/RAMP: PASSING SOLUTION

This solution provides a simple, straightforward method of meeting all the program requirements. All ramp and stair dimensions are properly established, and there is enough clearance at the side of the door for accessibility.

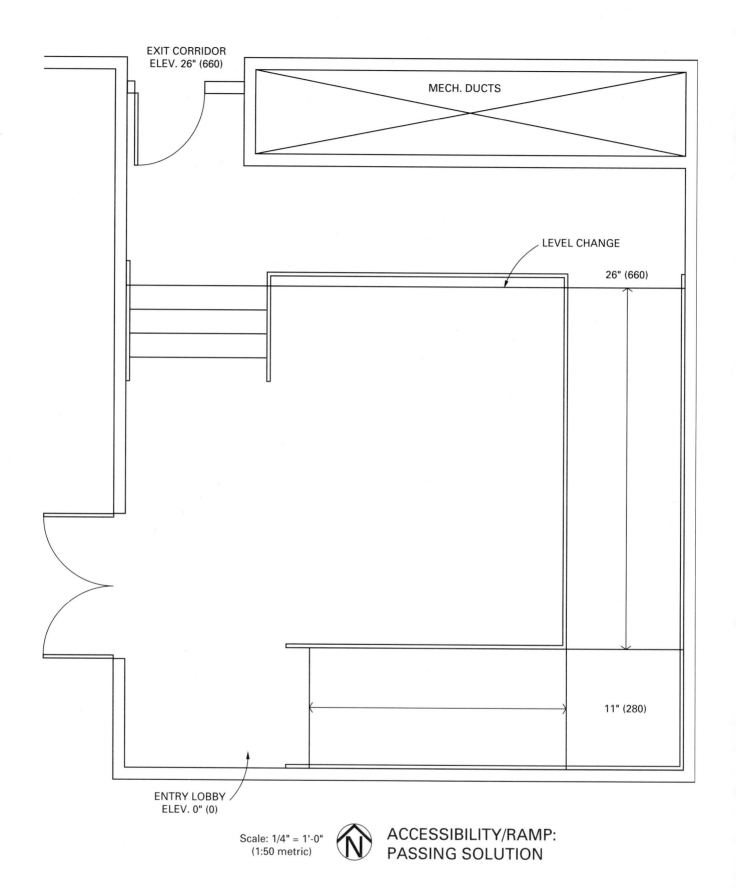

EXIT CORRIDOR
ELEV. 26" (660)

MECH. DUCTS

LEVEL CHANGE

26" (660)

11" (280)

ENTRY LOBBY
ELEV. 0" (0)

Scale: 1/4" = 1'-0"
(1:50 metric)

ACCESSIBILITY/RAMP:
PASSING SOLUTION

ACCESSIBILITY/RAMP: FAILING SOLUTION

This poor solution has a basic layout that would work if a few problems were corrected. The ramp landing is only 4 ft (1220) deep, which is less than the required 60 in (1525). The stairway is wider than it needs to be, which would be acceptable if an intermediate handrail had been shown. Also, there is no extension of the handrail on the west side of the stair. Finally, because the door is centered in the opening, the strike side of the door does not meet the 18 in (457) accessibility requirement.

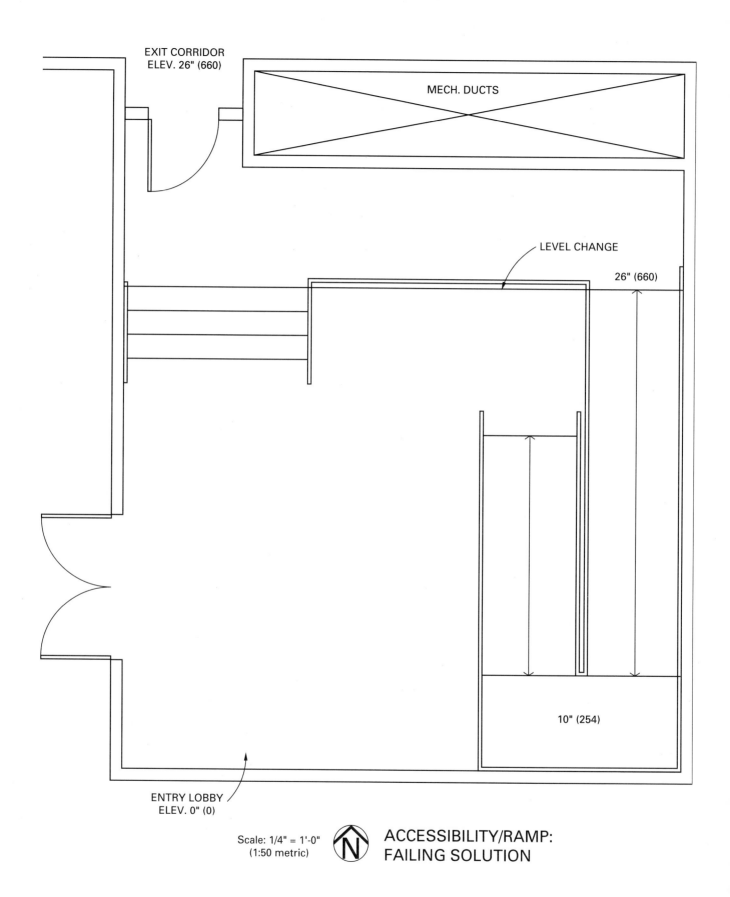

EXIT CORRIDOR
ELEV. 26" (660)

MECH. DUCTS

LEVEL CHANGE

26" (660)

10" (254)

ENTRY LOBBY
ELEV. 0" (0)

Scale: 1/4" = 1'-0"
(1:50 metric)

N

ACCESSIBILITY/RAMP:
FAILING SOLUTION

ROOF PLAN VIGNETTE

Directions

The roof system of a small visitors' center is shown. The outermost edges of two roofs are indicated by dashed lines. The higher roof is over the information/display areas, and the lower roof covers the remainder of the building. Configure these roofs for the effective removal of rainwater, satisfying the following requirements and the Roof Plan vignette program. Use the symbols shown in the Roof Plan legend.

1. Confine the solution to the areas defined by the dashed lines. Do not use eaves or overhangs.

2. For each roof area, define the extent, slope, and spot elevations of a plane or planes designed to remove rainwater using only roof slope, gutter, and downspouts. The outside edges of the roof planes must coincide with the dashed lines indicating the outermost edges of the roofs.

3. Indicate the locations of all necessary gutters and downspouts using the appropriate symbols.

4. Indicate the location of the clerestory.

5. Locate on the roof the HVAC condensing unit and any necessary plumbing vent stacks, skylights, and exhaust fans.

6. Show any necessary flashing and crickets.

7. Set the top of the roof elevation at the low points of the roof, and indicate roof slopes.

Program

General

1. The building consists of one volume over the information/display area, which must have a high roof, and one volume over the remainder of the building, which must have a low roof.

2. The information/display area must have a continuous clerestory window along the north side. The clerestory is to be 30 in (760) high, including the head and sill framing.

Roof Drainage

1. Only roof slope, gutters, and downspouts are to be used for removal of rainwater.

2. Rainwater should not discharge from the edge of an upper roof directly onto a lower roof or from any roof or gutter directly onto the ground.

3. Downspouts should not conflict with any door, window, or clerestory.

Construction

1. The finished floor elevation is 0 ft 0 in (0). The ceiling height under the lower roof is 8 ft 0 in (2440).

2. Every roof area must have a slope.

3. The roof over the information/display area shall have a slope between 6:12 and 10:12.

4. The roof over the remainder of the building must have a slope between 3:12 and 5:12.

5. The roof and structural assembly for both roofs is a total of 18 in (460).

6. Flashing must be provided at all roof/wall intersections. HVAC condensing units, plumbing vent stacks, and exhaust fans are self-flashing and require no additional flashing or crickets.

Mechanical

1. The HVAC condensing unit must be placed on a roof with a slope of 5:12 or less.

2. Place the HVAC condensing unit over a corridor and not closer than 5 ft 0 in (1525) from the roof edge.

3. Provide one exhaust fan for each toilet room.

Legend

The symbols to be used are shown in the legend.

Tips

- Use the *check* tool to ensure that roof planes are within the given limits of the roof.

- When roof planes meet, the lines indicating the edges must coincide.

- On the actual exam, to see the limits of the roof, turn off the *Display floorplan* option under the *layers* menu.

- On the actual exam, check for overlaps while working by using the *check* icon on the screen.

- If one element of two overlapping elements cannot be selected, keep clicking without moving the mouse until the desired element is highlighted.

Warnings

- The dashed lines labeled "edge of roof" are the outer limits of the roof. Do not extend the roof beyond these lines.

- Gutters and downspouts may be placed beyond the outer limits of the roof.

Tools

Useful tools include the following.

- *zoom* tool for checking the position of roof planes
- *set roof* tool to make calculating a roof elevation easier
- full-screen cursor to assist in aligning roof planes with the given roof edges

Target Time: 1 hour

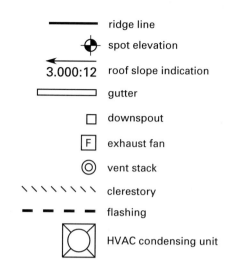

ROOF PLAN LEGEND

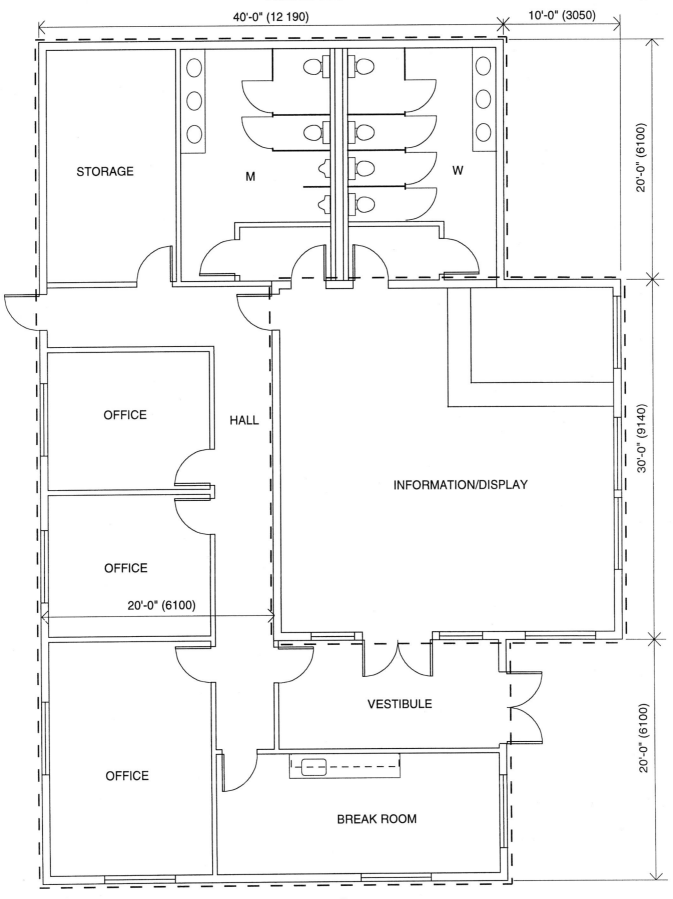

40'-0" (12 190)   10'-0" (3050)

20'-0" (6100)

30'-0" (9140)

20'-0" (6100)

STORAGE

M   W

OFFICE   HALL

OFFICE

20'-0" (6100)

INFORMATION/DISPLAY

OFFICE

VESTIBULE

BREAK ROOM

Scale: 1/8" = 1'-0"
(1:100 metric)

ROOF PLAN

ROOF PLAN: PASSING SOLUTION

This solution represents a simple, straightforward roof plan that sheds water effectively and includes all the required elements. The low portions of the lower roof are set at 9 ft 6 in (2895), which allows for the 18 in (457) structural depth. The slope meets the program limitations and still provides for adequate space for the 30 in (760) high clerestory. All water drains into gutters, which connect to properly located downspouts.

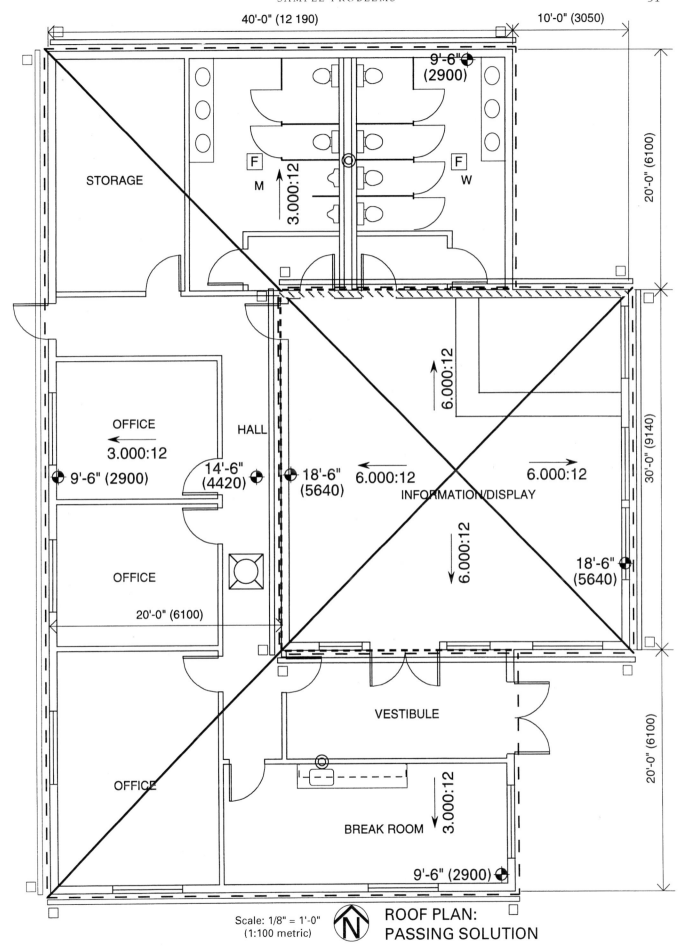

40'-0" (12 190)   10'-0" (3050)

9'-6"
(2900)

20'-0" (6100)

STORAGE

F   F
M   W

3.000:12

6.000:12

30'-0" (9140)

OFFICE   HALL

3.000:12   6.000:12   6.000:12

9'-6" (2900)   14'-6"   18'-6"   INFORMATION/DISPLAY
                (4420)   (5640)

OFFICE   6.000:12   18'-6"
                                                      (5640)

20'-0" (6100)

OFFICE   VESTIBULE

                                                      20'-0" (6100)

                          3.000:12

BREAK ROOM

9'-6" (2900)

Scale: 1/8" = 1'-0"   N   ROOF PLAN:
(1:100 metric)   PASSING SOLUTION

PPI • www.ppi2pass.com

ROOF PLAN: FAILING SOLUTION

The gable roof layout for this solution is adequate, but the elevations are set incorrectly. First, the 8 ft 0 in (2440) lower elevation of the lower roof does not allow for roof structure. Second, the lower roof slope and the elevation of the lower portion of the upper roof structure do not allow sufficient room for the clerestory and upper roof structure. Third, gutters are missing to catch rainwater draining from the upper roof to the lower roof. Finally, the vent for the break room sink is missing.

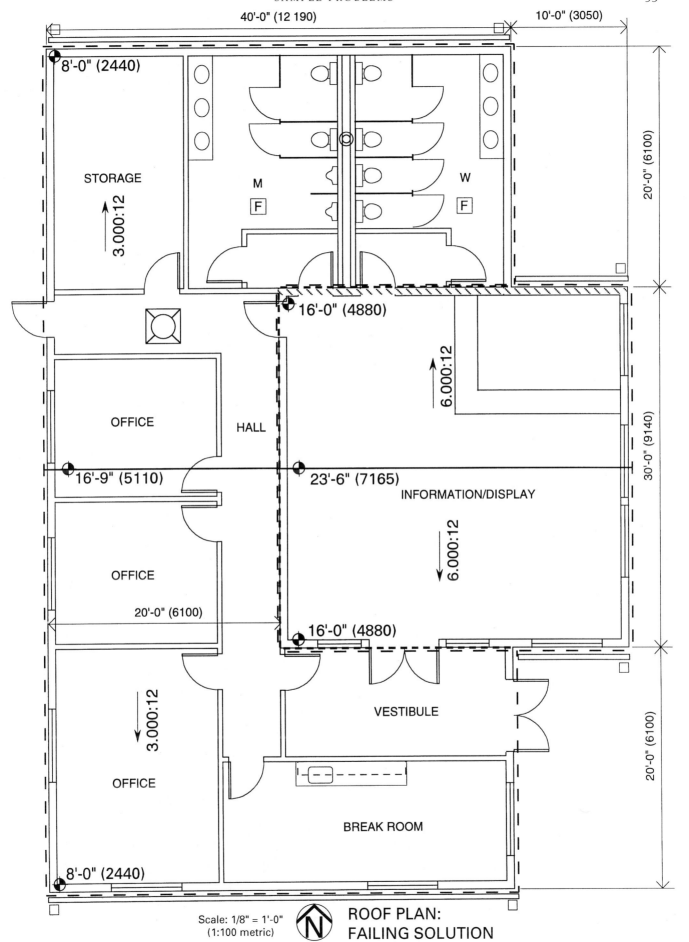

40'-0" (12 190)

10'-0" (3050)

8'-0" (2440)

20'-0" (6100)

STORAGE

3.000:12

M

F

W

F

16'-0" (4880)

6.000:12

OFFICE

HALL

16'-9" (5110)

23'-6" (7165)

INFORMATION/DISPLAY

6.000:12

OFFICE

20'-0" (6100)

16'-0" (4880)

30'-0" (9140)

3.000:12

VESTIBULE

20'-0" (6100)

OFFICE

8'-0" (2440)

BREAK ROOM

Scale: 1/8" = 1'-0"
(1:100 metric)

ROOF PLAN:
FAILING SOLUTION

N

PPI • www.ppi2pass.com

STAIR DESIGN VIGNETTE

Directions

On the base floor plans provided, design an exit stairway for an existing two-story building with a maintenance office located at a third level slightly above the first floor as shown in the section drawing. The design must provide a means of egress from the second floor and from the maintenance office to the door leading to the public way on the first floor. Draw the stairway, including all required handrails and guardrails. Indicate the elevations of all stair flights, at the top of the highest tread and at the bottom of the lowest riser, to match adjacent landing elevations.

Program

A new stairway is being designed to meet accessibility standards and increased occupant loads for an existing building. The design for the other building exit has already been completed.

The total occupant load and the number of exits for each level of the building are as follows.

building level	total occupant load	no. of exits
first floor	340	2
maintenance office	3	1
second floor	340	2

The stairway must provide a means of egress from all three levels and must provide a continuous path from the second floor to the first floor exit. The stairs will be constructed of precast concrete components that have landings 12 in (305) thick and stair flights 12 in (305) thick measured from the stair nosing to the soffit below.

The design must comply with the following code requirements.

Code Requirements

Comply with the following code requirements. These are the *only* code-related criteria required.

Capacity of Exit Components

1. The occupant load for each exit shall be determined by dividing the total occupant load for an individual floor by the number of exits serving that floor.

2. Where stairways serve more than one level, the capacity of the exit components shall be based on the individual floor with the largest occupant load, provided that the exit capacity shall not decrease in the direction of the means of egress.

3. The width of each exit component in inches shall not be less than the occupant load served by an exit multiplied by 0.3 in/person and shall not be less than the minimum width specified by this code.

Stairways

1. The minimum width shall be computed in accordance with the requirements for Capacity of Exit Components but shall not be less than 44 in (1120).

2. Projections into a required stairway are prohibited, except for handrail projections.

3. The minimum dimensions of landings shall not be less than the required width of the stairs.

4. On any given flight of stairs, all steps shall have uniform riser heights and uniform tread depths. Stair treads shall be no less than 11 in (280) deep measured from riser to riser. Stair risers shall be no more than 7 in (180) and no less than 4 in (100).

5. The minimum headroom of all parts of a stairway shall be not less than 80 in (2030) measured vertically from the tread nosing or from any floor surface, including landings.

Handrails

1. Stairways shall have handrails on both sides.

2. Handrails shall be continuous within the full length of each stair flight. The inside handrail on switchback and dogleg stairs shall be continuous.

3. If stair handrails are not continuous, at least one handrail shall extend at least 12 in (305) beyond the top and bottom risers.

4. Stairways more than 88 in (2235) wide shall have intermediate handrails.

Guardrails

Open sides of landings, floor surfaces, and stairways shall be protected by a continuous guardrail.

Doors

1. When opening, a door shall not reduce the width of a landing to less than half the required width.

2. There shall be a floor or landing on each side of a door, and the floor surface on both sides of the door shall be at the same elevation.

Area of Refuge

1. An accessible area of refuge serving the second floor shall be provided within the stair enclosure.

2. The area of refuge shall be sized to accommodate one wheelchair space of 30 in by 48 in (760 by 1220) for each 150 occupants or portion thereof, based on the stairway occupant load. Such spaces shall not reduce the required stair or landing width.

Tips

- Read the program and code requirements carefully.
- Calculate the number of risers needed before beginning the stair layout. On the actual exam, the draw stairs tool will provide a prompt to enter how many risers should be drawn. The tread depth is automatically calculated as the stairs are drawn.
- Calculate the minimum width of egress before beginning the stair layout.
- Draw elements on the correct layer as indicated by the ground floor cut line in the section drawing.
- If one element of two overlapping elements cannot be selected, keep clicking without moving the mouse until the desired element is highlighted.

Warnings

- The elevations of the stair and the landings must both be indicated, even if the elevations are the same.
- On the actual exam, if a stair or a landing in a given location is not drawn, the scoring mechanism assumes that the area is open to the space below.

Tools

Useful tools include the following.

- *zoom* tool for drawing stairs and handrails
- full-screen cursor to help line up elements

Target Time: 1 hour

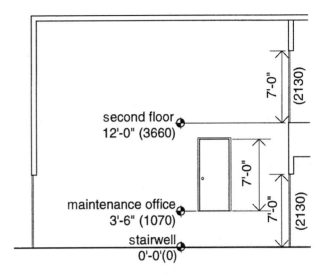

SECTION A-A

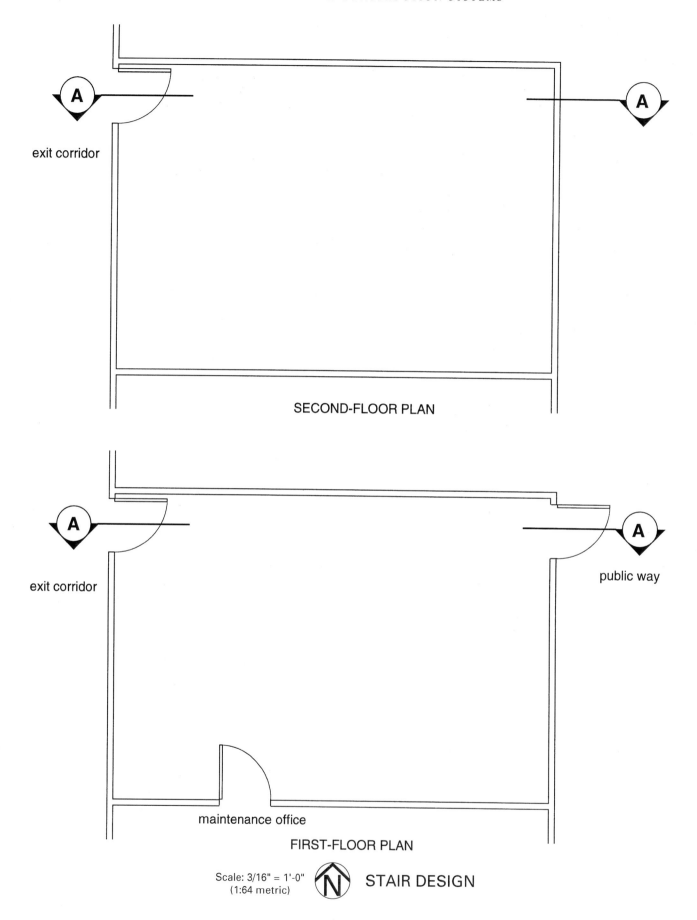

exit corridor

SECOND-FLOOR PLAN

exit corridor

public way

maintenance office

FIRST-FLOOR PLAN

Scale: 3/16" = 1'-0"
(1:64 metric)

STAIR DESIGN

STAIR DESIGN: PASSING SOLUTION

This solution meets all the program requirements. One of the first things to check with this vignette is the minimum width of the exit stairs. It may be the minimum width stated, but more often, the width must be calculated based on occupant load. The program states that the second-floor occupant load is 340 with two exits, which means that the second-floor exit must accommodate 170 people. Multiplying this by the 0.3 in/person factor as stated in the program gives a minimum width of 51 in or 4 ft 3 in (1295). Another thing to remember is to set the elevations of the tops and bottoms of all flights of stairs and of the landings themselves. Because the occupant load is over 150, two areas of refuge are required.

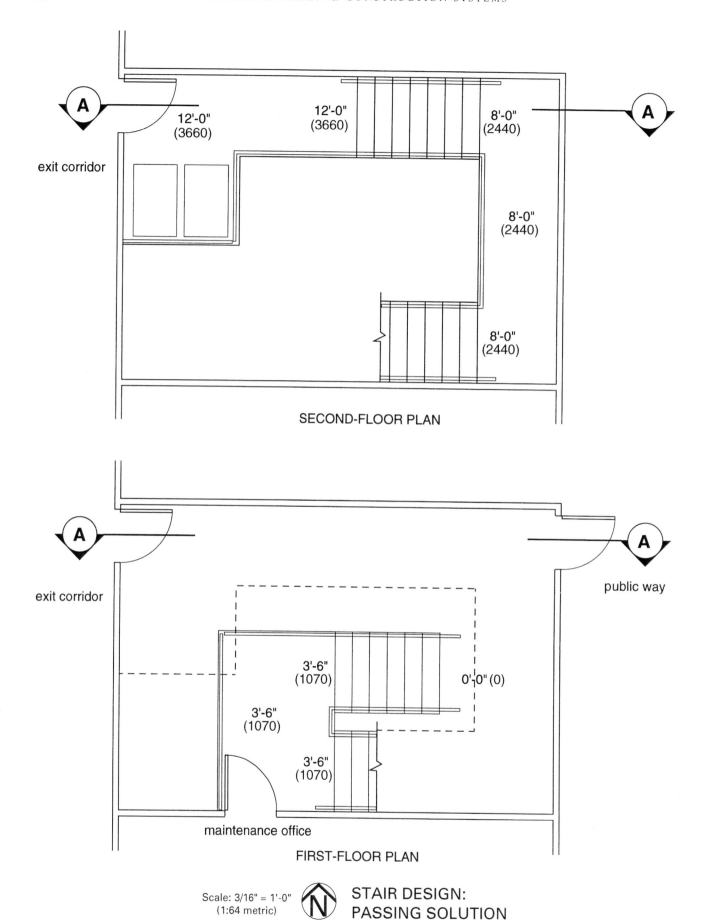

SECOND-FLOOR PLAN

FIRST-FLOOR PLAN

Scale: 3/16" = 1'-0"
(1:64 metric)

STAIR DESIGN:
PASSING SOLUTION

STAIR DESIGN: FAILING SOLUTION

This solution illustrates some of the common mistakes made in this vignette. The landing at 7 ft 6 in (2290) is a little too low for adequate headroom below. Because the program states that the precast structure is 12 in (305) deep, this would leave headroom of 6 ft 6 in (1980), which is 2 in (50) short of the minimum 80 in (2030). There is also no handrail on the north side of the upper flight of stairs.

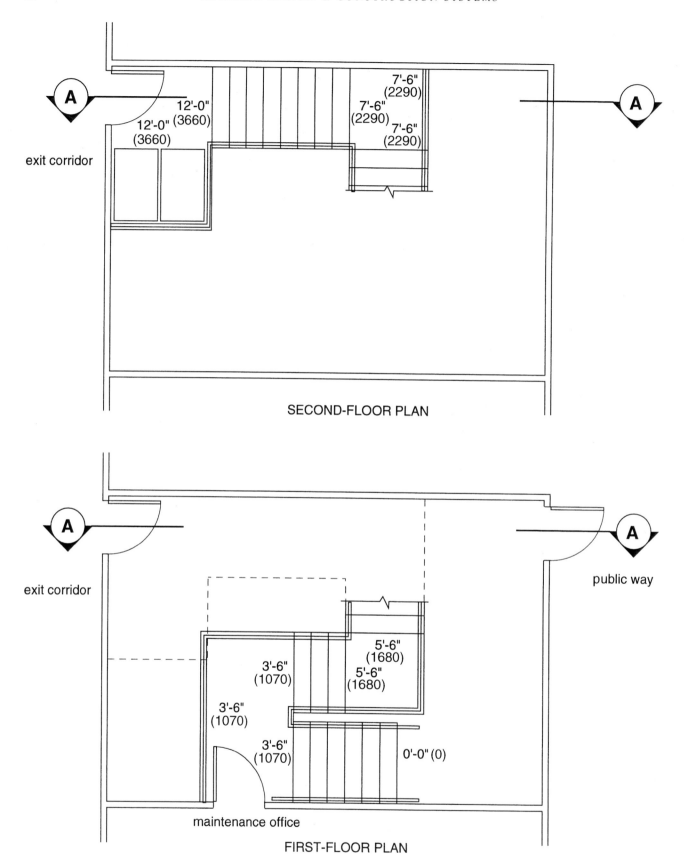

SECOND-FLOOR PLAN

FIRST-FLOOR PLAN

Scale: 3/16" = 1'-0"
(1:64 metric)

STAIR DESIGN:
FAILING SOLUTION

1. Proctor testing (ASTM D1557-02e1) is used to determine a soil's

    A. composition
    B. optimal density achievable, considering its moisture content
    C. ability when saturated to drain a given quantity of water in a specified period of time
    D. bearing capacity

2. Which of the following are considered stable soils? (Choose the two that apply.)

    A. clay
    B. gravel
    C. peat
    D. sand
    E. silt
    F. topsoil

3. In which of these locations must footings be placed?

    A. on bedrock
    B. at least 1 ft (305) below the frost line
    C. below the water table
    D. at the same depth throughout the building

4. The ground surrounding a building's foundation must be graded to slope away from the building. What is the minimum slope?

    A. $1/8$ in/ft (10 mm/m)
    B. $1/4$ in/ft (20 mm/m)
    C. $1/2$ in/ft (40 mm/m)
    D. 1 in/ft (80 mm/m)

5. Soils testing is performed on a project site and reveals a suitable bearing stratum at a depth of 100 ft (30 m). The composition of the soil is silt, clay, and sand. The water table is 10 ft (3 m) below the surface. Which of these foundation strategies is the best choice?

    A. friction piles
    B. concrete footings and CMU foundation walls with waterproofing
    C. end-bearing piles
    D. belled caissons

6. Which of the following is NOT a reason that a building's existing foundation may require underpinning?

    A. a change in building use from office space to warehouse
    B. plumbing leaks
    C. a change in building codes
    D. adjacent new construction

7. A 6 in (150) thick concrete slab is reinforced with no. 4 rebar placed in a horizontal grid and spaced 4 in (100) on center. The maximum size of the aggregate shall not exceed

    A. $1^1/2$ in (38)
    B. 1 in (25)
    C. 2 in (50)
    D. $2^5/8$ in (67)

8. The following are steps in the process of concrete construction. Put them in the correct order.

    I.   Apply a release agent to the forms.
    II.   Construct the formwork.
    III. Pour and vibrate the concrete.
    IV.   Place and tie the reinforcing steel.
    V.   Perform slump testing.

    A. II, IV, I, V, III
    B. II, I, IV, III, V
    C. II, I, IV, V, III
    D. V, II, I, IV, III

9. The chemical reaction that causes concrete to harden is known as

    A. oxidation
    B. evaporation
    C. hydration
    D. reduction

10. The application of epoxy-coated reinforcing bars would NOT be specified in

    A. a parking garage
    B. a fishing pier on the ocean
    C. an interior column in an office building
    D. an exterior concrete staircase

11.   What are the specified dimensions of a U.S. modular brick, as shown in the following illustration?

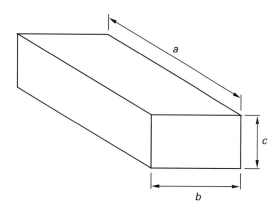

A. $a = 11^5/_8$ in (295), $b = 3^5/_8$ in (92), $c = 3^5/_8$ in (92)

B. $a = 7^5/_8$ in (194), $b = 3^5/_8$ in (92), $c = 2^1/_4$ in (57)

C. $a = 7^5/_8$ in (194), $b = 3^5/_8$ in (92), $c = 2^3/_4$ in (70)

D. $a = 11^5/_8$ in (295), $b = 3^5/_8$ in (92), $c = 2^1/_4$ in (57)

12.   Devices that hold reinforcing steel in position and prevent the rebar from slipping out of place as concrete is placed are called

A.   props
B.   lifts
C.   shims
D.   chairs

13.   To achieve a slip-resistant finish on a concrete floor slab, the architect should specify a

A.   float finish
B.   broom finish
C.   hard steel-troweled finish
D.   light steel-troweled finish

14.   A joint that is typically used where an addition meets an existing building to allow the two sections to move independently of one another is called

A.   a control joint
B.   a construction joint
C.   an expansion joint
D.   an isolation joint

15.   What type of mortar should be specified for a CMU foundation wall?

A.   M
B.   N
C.   O
D.   S

16.   What type of brick should be specified for the exterior of a project in Maine?

A.   FW
B.   NW
C.   MW
D.   SW

17.   Which mortar joint is NOT recommended for exterior use?

A.   concave
B.   flush
C.   vee
D.   raked

18.   Where should weep holes be located in a brick wall?

A.   at the lowest course of brick
B.   above windows
C.   above shelf angles
D.   at all of the above locations

19.   Rehabilitation of a building constructed in the 1860s requires cleaning and repairing the existing brick exterior walls. The brick is in good condition but is very dirty. Portions of the mortar have fallen out, and much of what remains is so soft that it can be scraped away with a fingernail. Which restoration technique should the architect recommend?

A.   pressure washing with a 10% muratic acid solution
B.   pressure washing with plain water and repointing the mortar
C.   hand washing the brick with water and a stiff brush and repointing the mortar
D.   sandblasting

20.   Limestone is an example of which of the following types of rock?

    A.   igneous
    B.   sedimentary
    C.   metamorphic
    D.   monumental

21.   Plywood used as sheathing is designated 32/16. What does this mean?

    A.   It is $1/2$ in thick.
    B.   It can be used to span rafters spaced at 32 in on center and joists spaced at 16 in on center.
    C.   It can support 32 lbf/ft^2 on joists placed at 16 in on center.
    D.   It can be used as sheathing for studs spaced at 16 in on center.

22.   The type of lockset that is most secure is a

    A.   unit lock
    B.   cylindrical lock
    C.   rim lock
    D.   mortise lock

23.   Identify the check rail on the pair of double-hung windows shown.

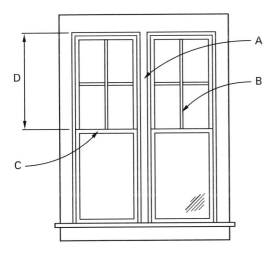

24.   Calculate the equivalent thickness of a 12 in (305) concrete block that is 75% solids.

    A. $8^1/_2$ in (216)
    B. $8^3/_4$ in (222)
    C.   9 in (229)
    D. $9^1/_4$ in (235)

25.   Calculate the skewback for the jack arch shown. The wall is two wythes thick.

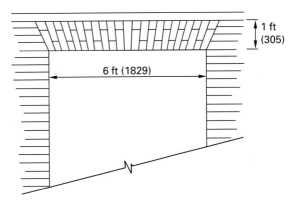

    A.   6 in (152)
    B.   8 in (203)
    C.   9 in (228)
    D.   12 in (305)

26.   A university is choosing between plastic laminate and solid-surface countertops for student apartments. A typical countertop is 8 linear ft (2 m) long.

The installation cost for the plastic laminate countertop is $60/linear ft ($200/m). The life span of a plastic laminate countertop under the heavy-use conditions found in student housing is about 10 years; after each 10-year period, the countertops will need to be replaced. The first replacement (after 10 years) is projected to cost $70/linear ft ($240/m). The second replacement (after 20 years) is projected to cost $80/linear ft ($270/m).

The installation cost for the solid-surface countertops is $110/linear ft ($370/m). Every 10 years the countertops will need to be refinished. The first refinishing (after 10 years) is projected to cost $10/linear ft ($30/m). The second refinishing (after 20 years) is projected to cost $20/linear ft ($60/m).

Which material's life-cycle cost will be lower over a 25-year period?

    A. plastic laminate

    B. solid surface

    C. the costs are the same

    D. impossible to determine from the information given

27.   What type of weld does the following symbol represent?

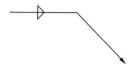

    A. V-groove weld with back-up bar

    B. double-bevel groove weld

    C. double-fillet weld

    D. fillet weld all around

28.   Which of the following is NOT a concrete test?

    A. Steiner tunnel test

    B. cylinder test

    C. electrical impedance test

    D. Kelly ball test

29.   According to model codes, which of the following are considered parts of the means of egress? (Choose the three that apply.)

    A. common path of travel

    B. exit

    C. exit access

    D. exit discharge

    E. public way

    F. travel distance

30.   Normal-slope asphalt or fiberglass shingles must be installed on a roof with a pitch of at least _____:12. (Fill in the blank.)

31.   Which is the correct location for a vapor retarder in a cold climate?

    A.

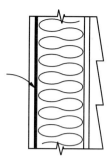

    B.

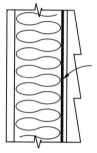

    C.

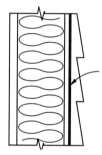

    D.

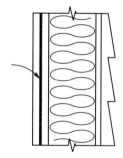

32. Which of these are important considerations in designing a fire-rated ceiling? (Choose the two that apply.)

    A. hold-down clips
    B. the structural slab
    C. thermal insulation
    D. the composition of the floor/ceiling assembly
    E. sound absorption
    F. the style of grid

33. When specifying a hardwood floor over a concrete slab on grade, which of the following should the architect also specify?

    A. ³/₄ in (19) plywood subflooring and 15# building felt
    B. ³/₄ in (19) tongue-and-groove plywood placed over a layer of mastic
    C. treated wood sleepers on mastic and a layer of polyethylene vapor barrier
    D. 15# building felt

34. The average *R*-value per inch of fiberglass batt insulation is _____. (Fill in the blank.)

35. Which of the following woods must be treated for resistance to decay when used in an exterior application?

    A. cedar
    B. spruce
    C. redwood
    D. cypress

36. Aluminum windows are specified for installation in a masonry wall. Which material is the least desirable choice for flashing at the head of the window?

    A. aluminum
    B. copper
    C. stainless steel (passive)
    D. lead

37. What is the significance of Burnham and Root's Reliance Building, built in Chicago and completed in 1895?

    A. It features load-bearing masonry walls at the perimeter that support an interior frame of iron.
    B. It was the first building to be clad completely with a curtain-wall structure.
    C. It features curtain walls and large "Chicago-style" windows, and its facade expresses the pattern of the building's structural frame.
    D. The lower levels of the building feature elaborately detailed cast-iron ornament.

38. Which mid-twentieth-century architect was known for his use of concrete, masonry, and interplay with natural light?

    A. Ludwig Mies van der Rohe
    B. Le Corbusier
    C. Louis I. Kahn
    D. Frank Lloyd Wright

39. An architect is designing custom oak cabinetry and wants the grain of the door frames to be as straight and consistent as possible. Which type of sawing should be specified?

    A. plain sawing
    B. quarter sawing
    C. flat sawing
    D. rift sawing

40. Which is typically the most expensive type of cabinetry construction?

    A. flush
    B. flush overlay
    C. reveal overlay
    D. lipped overlay

41. Which of the following statements is true?

    A. Dampproofing controls moisture that is under hydrostatic pressure.
    B. Membrane coatings should always be used for dampproofing.
    C. Waterproofing membranes may be easily punctured and require a protective covering.
    D. If hydrostatic pressure is present, foundation drains will be of no use.

42. When planning an accessible bathroom, how much space should be allowed for a standard roll-in-type shower and its required clear floor space as described in the *ADA/ABA Guidelines*?

    A.   30 in (760) by 60 in (1525)
    B.   36 in (915) by 60 in (1525)
    C.   48 in (1219) by 60 in (1525)
    D.   60 in (1525) by 60 in (1525)

43. An architect has been asked to design an office suite for the president of a major company. The president often holds confidential meetings in his office and requests a design that limits sound transmission to the surrounding corridor. Which of the following is the most important acoustical strategy to include in the design?

    A.   Build walls with staggered studs and mount the gypsum board on resilient channels.
    B.   Extend the partitions from deck to deck and provide acoustical seals at the top and bottom of the walls.
    C.   Provide unfaced batt insulation in the partitions between the office and the corridor.
    D.   Specify absorptive finish materials such as carpeting, draperies, and acoustical tile.

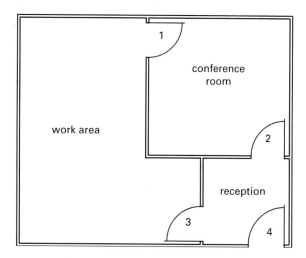

44. In the following illustration, what is the hand of door 3?

    A.   RHR
    B.   RH
    C.   LHR
    D.   LH

45. Which of the following is a UL-rated 2-hour wall assembly?

A.

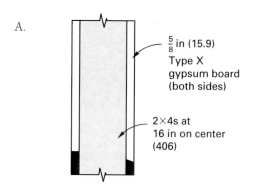

B.

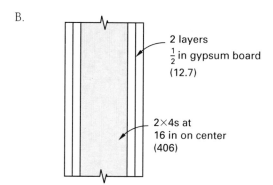

C.

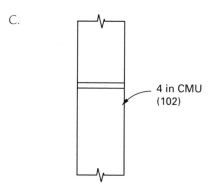

D.

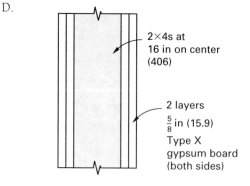

46. Which of the following materials is NOT considered a rapidly renewable building material?

    A. chestnut flooring sawn from old barn beams
    B. wheat board cabinetry
    C. linoleum
    D. bamboo paneling

47. Identify the following critical dimensions as required by the *ADA/ABA Guidelines*.

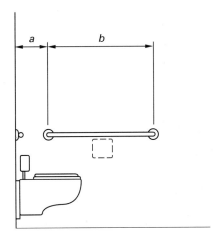

    A. $a = 6$ in (153) minimum, $b = 42$ in (1065) minimum
    B. $a = 12$ in (305) maximum, $b = 42$ in (1065) minimum
    C. $a = 12$ in (305) maximum, $b = 48$ in (1219) minimum
    D. $a = 6$ in (153) minimum, $b = 48$ in (1219) minimum

48. Which of the following would NOT provide lateral stability?

    A. diagonal bracing
    B. 2×4s spaced at 12 in (305) on center
    C. plywood sheathing
    D. steel rods with turnbuckles

49. Classify the structural steel shape shown.

    A. W shape
    B. I shape
    C. S shape
    D. H shape

50. Which of the following are characteristics of stainless steel? (Choose the three that apply.)

    A. It cannot be welded.
    B. It should not be in contact with copper.
    C. It is an alloy of steel and chromium.
    D. It is only available with mechanical and coated finishes.
    E. It corrodes easily if exposed to oxygen.
    F. It is approximately as strong as bronze.

51. What are the minimum dimensions permitted for the hearth shown? The height of the fireplace opening is 24 in (610).

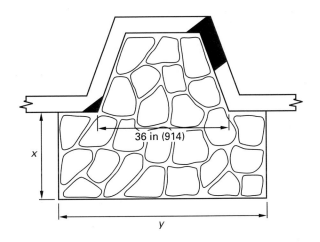

    A. $x = 16$ in (406), $y = 48$ in (1219)
    B. $x = 20$ in (508), $y = 52$ in (1320)
    C. $x = 24$ in (610), $y = 48$ in (1219)
    D. $x = 24$ in (610), $y = 52$ in (1320)

52. Identify the following brick positions. (The exterior face is shaded.)

I.

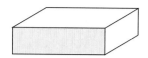

II.

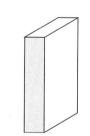

III.

IV.

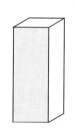

    A. I–stretcher, II–soldier, III–rowlock, IV–sailor
    B. I–stretcher, II–soldier, III–header, IV–sailor
    C. I–shiner, II–sailor, III–rowlock, IV–soldier
    D. I–shiner, II–sailor, III–header, IV–soldier

53. The structural member shown in the following illustration is known as a

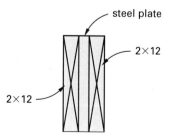

    A. composite beam
    B. flitch beam
    C. built-up beam
    D. sistered beam

54. An old warehouse is being converted into an apartment building. The project will be seeking LEED certification, so a high priority will be placed on sustainable design. Which of the following existing building elements is least likely to be reused?

    A. masonry walls
    B. heavy timber framing
    C. roof framing members
    D. windows

55. According to the size groups of yard lumber, a 6 in (152) by 8 in (203) member would be classified as a

    A. board
    B. post
    C. beam
    D. timber

56. The energy required to turn a raw material into a finished building product is known as

    A. manufacturing energy
    B. embodied energy
    C. production energy
    D. commissioning energy

57. The portion of the roof indicated at A is a

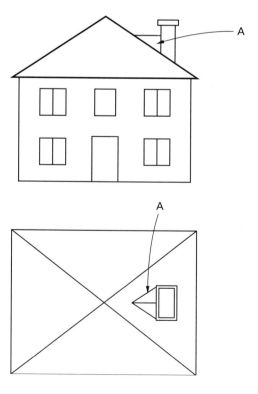

A. cricket

B. hip

C. gable

D. dormer

58. Which of the following is laminated glass commonly used for? (Choose the four that apply.)

A. acoustical control

B. decorative purposes

C. fire protection

D. insulation

E. safety

F. security

59. Auguste Perret is known for his skill in creating buildings using

A. masonry

B. reinforced concrete

C. steel

D. iron

60. During which period in the curing process does concrete gain the most compressive strength?

A. 0 to 3 days

B. 3 to 7 days

C. 7 to 14 days

D. 14 to 28 days

61. Which of the following paving materials has the lowest albedo?

A. asphalt

B. concrete made with gray cement

C. concrete made with white cement

D. brick pavers

62. What is the most common method of splicing reinforcing bars in concrete?

A. welding

B. lapping

C. metal sleeves

D. cylinder connectors

63. Blocking that eases the transition between a roof deck and the parapet wall in a membrane roof installation is known as a

A. chamfer

B. cant

C. transition strip

D. scupper

64. Which of the following types of metal should NOT be specified for connection hardware and flashing for use with wood treated with ACQ preservative?

A. aluminum

B. copper

C. stainless steel

D. hot-dip galvanized

65. Triglyphs and metopes are elements of the

A. Doric order

B. Ionic order

C. Corinthian order

D. Classical order

66. Which of the following strategies will NOT prevent ice dams?

A. Provide ridge and soffit vents.

B. Place batt insulation between the roof rafters.

C. Seal and insulate ductwork in the attic space.

D. Caulk all penetrations from below, such as electrical conduit or vent stacks.

67. An architect has designed a bakery/coffee shop in Pittsburgh, Pennsylvania. The business is such a success that three years later, the owner decides to allow her sister, who lives in Durham, North Carolina, to open a similar store using the same name, logos, and decor. After consultation with the architect, they determine that a building of similar size and design will be appropriate for the Durham location. The sisters ask the architect for a rough projection of the cost to build the new bakery/coffee shop based upon the construction cost of the Pittsburgh store.

The location factor for Pittsburgh is 100. The cost factor for Durham is 75. The inflation rate has been 2% per year since the first building was built. The original construction cost was $300,000.

Based upon the information given, approximately how much will it cost to construct the new building?

    A. $225,000

    B. $239,000

    C. $306,000

    D. $318,000

68. Which CSI MasterFormat 2010 division includes polyisocyanurate?

    A. 03

    B. 05

    C. 07

    D. 09

69. An architect is designing an addition to a high school to house a new gym and locker rooms. The architect plans to construct the exterior walls with concrete masonry units and apply an exterior insulation and finish system (EIFS) over the block. The new gym will be located adjacent to the school's baseball field. To take advantage of the material's insulative properties and provide the best impact resistance to avoid dents from fly balls, which type of EIFS system should be specified?

    A. PB

    B. PM

    C. MB

    D. EPS

70. A contractor is calculating how much lumber he needs to order to build a small addition on a client's house. The three exterior walls are to be framed with 2×6 studs at 16 in (0.4 m) on center. The room is 12 ft (3.7 m) by 12 ft (3.7 m), so he estimates that he will need nine 8 ft (2.44 m) studs for each wall. The contractor will be charged by the board-foot for the lumber he purchases. How many board-feet will he need to buy?

    A. 108 board-feet

    B. 144 board-feet

    C. 216 board-feet

    D. 243 board-feet

71. An architect is designing a 10-story building and is analyzing the options for the cladding system. She has determined that the building will have a prefabricated curtain wall made of aluminum with a variety of glass vision and spandrel panels. Although the structural grid of the building is very regular, to add visual interest to the facade, the panels will be a variety of sizes. Which type of curtain-wall system would be the least desirable choice for this application?

    A. stick

    B. unit-and-mullion

    C. panel

    D. unit

72. Why are heavy timber beams chamfered?

    A. Chamfering provides a more elegant appearance.

    B. Chamfering allows a burning beam to rotate free of the masonry wall in a fire.

    C. Chamfering removes the part of the beam that can ignite most easily.

    D. Chamfering allows the pintle caps to fit correctly.

73. Which paint finish contains the greatest amount of pigment?

    A. flat

    B. satin

    C. semigloss

    D. gloss

74. The tolerance for the difference between riser heights or tread depths within a flight of stairs is

    A. 0 in (0)

    B. 0.25 in (6.35)

    C. 0.375 in (9.5)

    D. 0.50 in (12.7)

75. What is the most appropriate elevator speed for a four-story apartment building with a floor-to-floor height of 15 ft (4.6 m)?

    A. 200 ft/min (1.0 m/s)

    B. 250 ft/min (1.3 m/s)

    C. 350 ft/min (1.8 m/s)

    D. 450 ft/min (2.3 m/s)

76. What is the optimal minimum width of a center-opening door in a passenger elevator?

    A. 3 ft (914)

    B. 3 ft 6 in (1067)

    C. 4 ft (1219)

    D. 4 ft 6 in (1372)

77. Radon testing is conducted in the basement of an elementary school that is under study for a renovation and addition project. The results show a concentration of 3 pCi/L. Determine an appropriate course of action.

    A. Demolish the existing slab and install a new 4 in (102) slab on a vapor barrier placed on top of a 4 in (102) base course of gravel.

    B. Seal any cracks in the foundation walls and floor slab and ventilate the basement to the exterior.

    C. Install a membrane on the floor and ventilate beneath it.

    D. No action is required at this time, but the site should be monitored.

78. A small gasoline station, built in the 1930s along Route 66 in Missouri, has been left abandoned for 10 years. The new owners of the property want to fix it up and operate an automotive museum and small restaurant on the property. The building is listed on the National Register of Historic Places. The owners plan to apply for federal tax credits. According to the definitions established by the Secretary of the Interior's Standards for the Treatment of Historic Properties, which of the following treatments should be selected?

    A. preservation

    B. rehabilitation

    C. restoration

    D. reconstruction

79. The limits of an excavation and building footprint are located by a surveyor and marked using

    A. grade stakes

    B. batter boards

    C. corner pins

    D. a transit

80. The Eiffel Tower is built of

    A. wrought iron

    B. cast iron

    C. malleable iron

    D. steel

81. Typical 4 in (102) by 4 in (102) ceramic tiles used as wallcovering in an office building's restrooms should be specified as

    A. vitreous

    B. semivitreous

    C. nonvitreous

    D. impervious

82. Identify the architrave in the following illustration.

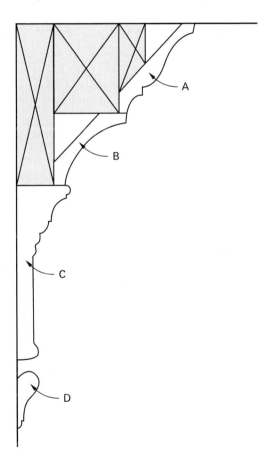

83. What type of plywood is used for roof sheathing?

    A. A-B Exterior
    B. B-C Exterior
    C. C-D Exterior
    D. A-D Exterior

84. Which of the following edge treatments for gypsum board does not require finishing with joint compound?

    A. LC bead
    B. L bead
    C. LK bead
    D. U bead

85. What type of elevator should be specified for a 40-story office building?

    A. hydraulic
    B. gearless traction
    C. geared traction
    D. electric

PRACTICE EXAM: VIGNETTES

Target Time: three vignettes in 2.75 hours

ACCESSIBILITY/RAMP

Directions

Develop a stair and ramp system and doorway to satisfy the program requirements and code restrictions for the base plan shown. Indicate all ramps, stairs, railings, walls, doors, and landings required to complete the plan.

Before beginning, review the program, code information, and the site plan.

Program

1. An existing building entrance is being remodeled to conform to egress and accessibility codes. Provide an accessible circulation system, including a ramp and stairway, to connect the lobby level with the sidewalk or to connect a plaza extension to the sidewalk.

2. Locate a wall and door on the upper level to create a new entry vestibule outside the lobby.

3. No portion of the ramp or stairs may encroach on the existing upper level or onto the sidewalk or pool.

4. Show the elevations of all new landings.

Code Requirements

Comply with the following code requirements. These are the *only* code-related criteria required.

General

1. The minimum width of an exit route shall not be less than 44 in (1120).

2. Projections into a required exit route width are prohibited, except for handrail projections.

3. The space required for a wheelchair to make a 180° turn is a clear space of 60 in (1525).

Stairs

1. The minimum width shall not be less than 60 in (1525).

2. Projections into a required stairway are prohibited, except for handrail projections.

3. The minimum dimension of landings measured in the direction of travel shall not be less than the width of the stairway.

4. On any given flight of stairs, all steps shall have uniform riser heights and uniform tread widths. Stair treads shall be no less than 11 in (280) wide, measured from riser to riser. Stair risers shall be no more than 7 in (180) and no less than 4 in (100).

Ramps

Any part of an accessible route with a slope greater than 1:20 shall be considered a ramp and shall comply with the following requirements.

1. The maximum slope of a ramp in new construction shall be 1:12. The maximum rise for any run shall be 30 in (760).

2. The minimum clear width of a ramp shall be 44 in (915). Projections into a required ramp width are prohibited, except for handrail projections.

3. Ramps shall have level landings at the bottom and top of each ramp run, at all points of turning, and at doors. Landings shall have the following features.

   - The landing shall be at least as wide as the ramp run leading to it.

   - The landing's minimum dimension in the direction of travel shall be 60 in (1525).

- If a ramp changes direction at a landing, the landing's minimum dimension shall be 60 in (1525) by 60 in (1525).

- If a doorway is located at a landing, the area in front of the doorway shall have maneuvering clearances as described in the code section on doors.

Handrails

1. Stairways and ramps shall have handrails on both sides. Exception: Handrails are not required on ramps where the vertical distance between landings is 6 in (150) or less.

2. Handrails shall be continuous within the full length of each ramp run and stair flight. The inside handrail on switchback and dogleg stairs and ramps shall be continuous.

3. If ramp handrails are not continuous, they shall extend at least 12 in (305) beyond the top and bottom of the ramp segment and shall be parallel with the floor or ground surface.

4. If stair handrails are not continuous, they shall extend at least 12 in (305) beyond the top and bottom risers.

5. Stairways more than 60 in (1525) wide shall have intermediate handrails.

Guardrails

Open sides of landings, floor surfaces, ramps, and stairways shall be protected by a continuous guardrail.

Doors

1. Doorways shall have a minimum clear opening of 32 in (815) with the door open 90°, measured between the face of the door and the opposite stop.

2. Exit doors shall swing in the direction of egress travel.

3. Minimum maneuvering clearances at doors shall be as shown.

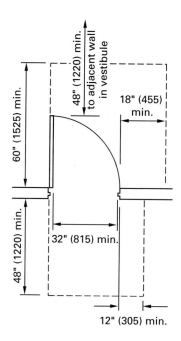

door maneuvering clearances

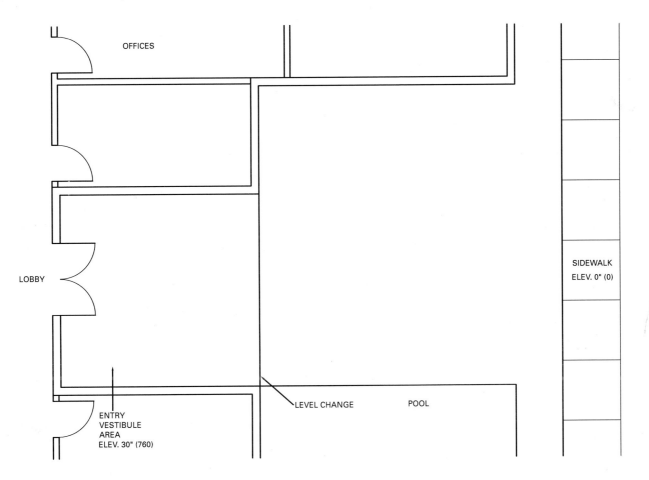

OFFICES

LOBBY

SIDEWALK
ELEV. 0" (0)

ENTRY
VESTIBULE
AREA
ELEV. 30" (760)

LEVEL CHANGE

POOL

Scale: 1/8" = 1'-0"
(1:100 metric)

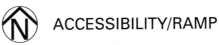

ACCESSIBILITY/RAMP

ROOF PLAN

Directions

The floor plan of a small alumni center is shown. The outermost edges of two roofs are indicated by dashed lines. Configure these roofs for the effective removal of rainwater, satisfying the following requirements and the program for this vignette. Use the symbols shown in the legend.

1. Confine the solution to the areas defined by the dashed lines. Do not use eaves or overhangs.

2. For each roof area, define the extent, slope, and spot elevations of a plane or planes designed to remove rainwater using only roof slope, gutter, and downspouts. The outside edges of the roof planes must coincide with the dashed lines indicating the outermost edges of the roofs.

3. Indicate the locations of all necessary gutters and downspouts using the appropriate symbols.

4. Indicate the location of the clerestory.

5. Locate on the roof the HVAC condensing unit and any necessary plumbing vent stacks, skylights, and exhaust fans.

6. Show any necessary flashing and crickets. Assume the chimney penetrates any roof plane drawn over it.

7. Set the roof elevation point at the low points of the roof, and indicate roof slopes toward the gutters. On the actual exam the elevation may be set at any corner of a roof polygon.

Program

General

1. The building consists of one volume over the event area, which must have a high roof, and one volume over the remainder of the building, which must have a low roof. Each volume has a roof height and slope requirement.

Roof Drainage

1. Only the roof slope, gutters, and downspouts are to be used for removal of rainwater.

2. Rainwater should not discharge from the edge of an upper roof directly onto a lower roof or from any roof or gutter directly onto the ground.

3. Downspouts should not conflict with any door, window, or clerestory.

Construction

1. The finished floor elevation is 0 ft 0 in (0). The ceiling height under the lower roof is 8 ft 0 in (2440).

2. All roof areas must have a slope.

3. The roof over the event area shall have a slope between 6:12 and 10:12.

4. The roof over the remainder of the building must have a slope between 2:12 and 5:12.

5. The roof and structural assembly for each roof is a total of 18 in (460) thick.

6. The event area must have a continuous clerestory window along the north side. The clerestory is to be 30 in (760) high. The clerestory sill and head framing are included in the overall height dimension.

7. Natural light must be provided for all rooms by means of windows, clerestory window, or skylight. Skylights must be provided only where no windows are shown and no clerestory window has been specified. Skylights are not required in halls, storage rooms, and closets.

8. Flashing must be provided at all roof/wall intersections. HVAC condensing units, skylights, plumbing vent stacks, and exhaust fans are self-flashing and require no additional flashing or crickets.

Mechanical

1. The HVAC condensing unit must be placed on a roof with a slope of 5:12 or less.

2. Place the HVAC condensing unit over a corridor and not closer than 5 ft 0 in (1525) from the roof edge. Do not place in front of the clerestory window.

3. Provide one exhaust fan for each toilet room.

4. Provide plumbing vent stacks through the roof where required to vent plumbing fixtures.

Legend

The symbols to be used are shown in the legend.

———————   ridge line

⊕   spot elevation

3.000:12   roof slope indication

▨▨▨▨   clerestory

━ ━   flashing

◎   vent stack

☐F   exhaust fan

▭   gutter

∘   downspout

△   cricket

⊠   skylight

⬚   HVAC condensing unit

ROOF PLAN LEGEND

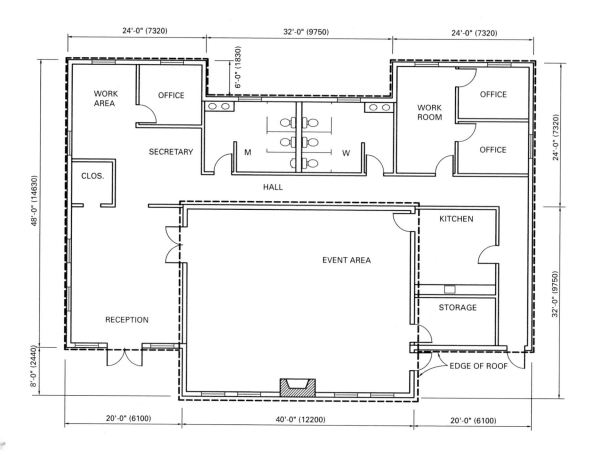

24'-0" (7320)   32'-0" (9750)   24'-0" (7320)

6'-0" (1830)

WORK AREA   OFFICE

OFFICE

WORK ROOM

OFFICE

SECRETARY   M   W

48'-0" (14630)   24'-0" (7320)

CLOS.

HALL

KITCHEN

EVENT AREA

RECEPTION   32'-0" (9750)

STORAGE

8'-0" (2440)   EDGE OF ROOF

20'-0" (6100)   40'-0" (12200)   20'-0" (6100)

Scale: 1/16" = 1'-0"   N   ROOF PLAN
(1:200 metric)

STAIR DESIGN

Directions

On the base floor plans provided, design an exit stairway for an existing three-level building. The exit on the ground level leads to the exterior and has a doorway to a mechanical room that also exits through the stairwell. The lower level of the building is slightly above the grade level as shown on the section drawing. The design must provide a means of egress using stairs from the second level and from the lower level to the exterior of the building on the grade level. Also, include the following.

- Indicate the elevations of all landings.
- Indicate the elevations of all stair flights, at the highest riser and at the bottom of the lowest riser, to match adjacent landing elevations.
- Indicate all handrails and guards.
- Connect the stair flights only to landings or the ground floor.

Before beginning, review the program, code information, floor plans, and the section.

Program

A new stairway is being designed to meet accessibility standards and increased occupant loads for an existing building. The design for the other building exit has already been completed.

The total occupant load and the number of exits for each level of the building are as follows.

building level	total occupant load	no. of exits
grade level	3	1
lower level	400	2
second level	320	2

The stairway must provide a means of egress from all three levels and must provide a continuous path from the second floor to the first floor exit. The stairs will be constructed of precast concrete components that have landings 12 in (305) thick and stair flights 12 in (305) thick measured from the stair nosing to the soffit below.

Code Requirements

Comply with the following code requirements. These are the *only* code-related criteria required.

Capacity of Exit Components

1. The occupant load for each exit shall be determined by dividing the total occupant load for an individual floor by the number of exits serving that floor.

2. Where a stairway serves more than one level, the capacity of the exit components shall be based on the individual floor with the largest occupant load, provided that the exit capacity shall not decrease in the direction of the means of egress.

3. The width of each exit component in inches shall not be less than the occupant load served by an exit multiplied by 0.3 in/person and shall not be less than the minimum width specified by this code.

Stairways

1. The minimum width shall be computed in accordance with the requirements for capacity of exit components, but shall not be less than 44 in (1120).

2. Projections into a required stairway are prohibited, except for handrail projections.

3. The minimum dimensions of landings shall not be less than the required width of the stairs.

4. On any given flight of stairs, all steps shall have uniform riser heights and uniform tread depths. Stair treads shall be no less than 11 in (280) deep measured from riser to riser. Stair risers shall be no more than 7 in (180) and no less than 4 in (100).

5. The minimum headroom at every part of a stairway shall not be less than 80 in (2030) measured vertically from the tread nosing and from any floor surface, including landings.

Handrails

1. Stairways shall have handrails on both sides.

2. Handrails shall be continuous within the full length of each stair flight. The inside handrail on switchback and dogleg stairs shall be continuous.

3. If stair handrails are not continuous, at least one handrail shall extend at least 12 in (305) beyond the top and bottom risers.

4. Stairways more than 88 in (2235) wide shall have intermediate handrails.

Guardrails

Open sides of landings, floor surfaces, and stairways shall be protected by a continuous guardrail.

Doors

1. When open, a door shall not reduce the width of a landing to less than half the required width.

2. There shall be a floor or landing on each side of a door, and the floor surface on both sides of the door shall be at the same elevation.

Area of Refuge

1. An accessible area of refuge serving upper levels shall be provided within the stair enclosure.

2. The area of refuge shall be sized to accommodate one wheelchair space of 30 in (760) by 48 in (1220) for each 175 occupants or portion thereof, based on the stairway occupant load. Such spaces shall not reduce the required stair or landing width.

3. When areas of refuge are required, stairway width shall have a minimum clear width of 48 in (1220) between handrails.

Tips

• Before drawing stairs, calculate how many risers are needed.

• When drawing treads, be careful to make sure the minimum depth is indicated. On the actual exam, the tread depth will be automatically calculated. The tread measurement is displayed in the element information area at the bottom of the work screen.

• Check for overlaps while working by using the check icon on the screen.

• If one element of two overlapping elements cannot be selected, keep clicking without moving the mouse until the desired element is highlighted.

Warnings

• Be sure to understand the existing elevations and indicate the new elevations of all landings.

Tools

Useful tools include the following.

• *zoom* tool for checking clearances and overlapping elements

• *sketch circle* tool to indicate required handrail extensions and door maneuvering clearances

• full-screen cursor to help line up elements

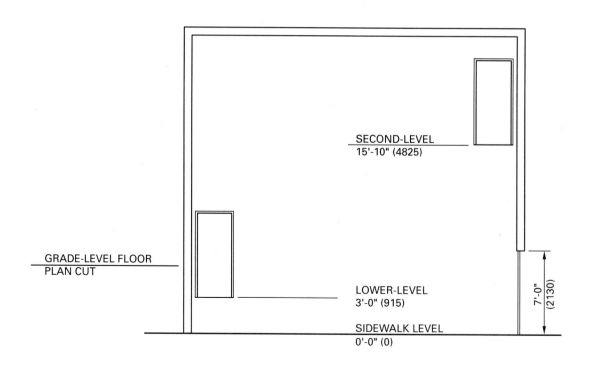

S-S

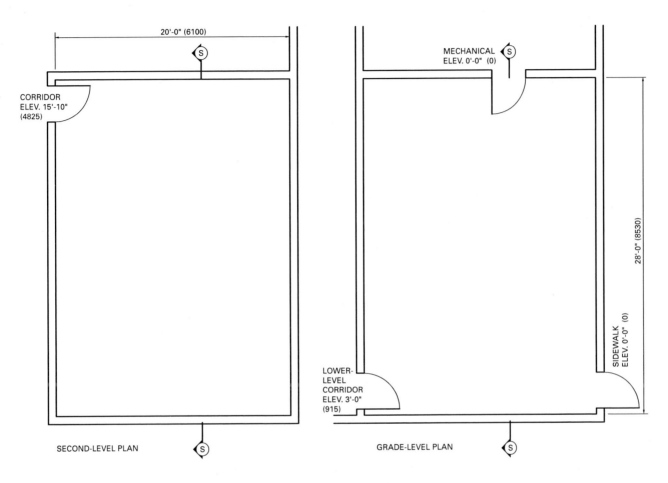

SECOND-LEVEL PLAN

GRADE-LEVEL PLAN

Scale: 1/8" = 1'-0"
(1:100 metric)

STAIR DESIGN

PRACTICE EXAM: MULTIPLE CHOICE SOLUTIONS

1. (A) ● (C) (D)
2. (A) ● (C) ● (E) (F)
3. (A) ● (C) (D)
4. (A) ● (C) (D)
5. ● (B) (C) (D)
6. (A) (B) ● (D)
7. (A) (B) ● (D)
8. (A) (B) ● (D)
9. (A) (B) ● (D)
10. (A) (B) ● (D)
11. (A) ● (C) (D)
12. (A) (B) (C) ●
13. (A) ● (C) (D)
14. (A) (B) (C) ●
15. ● (B) (C) (D)
16. (A) (B) (C) ●
17. (A) (B) (C) ●
18. (A) (B) (C) ●
19. (A) (B) ● (D)
20. (A) ● (C) (D)
21. (A) ● (C) (D)
22. (A) (B) (C) ●
23. (A) (B) ● (D)
24. (A) ● (C) (D)
25. (A) (B) ● (D)

26. (A) ● (C) (D)
27. (A) (B) ● (D)
28. ● (B) (C) (D)
29. (A) ● ● ● (E) (F)
30. _____ **4** _____
31. ● (B) (C) (D)
32. ● (B) (C) ● (E) (F)
33. (A) (B) ● (D)
34. _____ **3.3** _____
35. (A) ● (C) (D)
36. (A) (B) ● (D)
37. (A) (B) ● (D)
38. (A) (B) ● (D)
39. (A) (B) (C) ●
40. ● (B) (C) (D)
41. (A) (B) ● (D)
42. (A) (B) (C) ●
43. (A) ● (C) (D)
44. (A) (B) (C) ●
45. (A) (B) (C) ●
46. ● (B) (C) (D)
47. (A) ● (C) (D)
48. (A) ● (C) (D)
49. (A) (B) ● (D)
50. (A) ● ● ● (E) (F)

51. (A) ● (C) (D)
52. ● (B) (C) (D)
53. (A) ● (C) (D)
54. (A) (B) (C) ●
55. (A) (B) ● (D)
56. (A) ● (C) (D)
57. ● (B) (C) (D)
58. ● ● (C) (D) ● ●
59. (A) ● (C) (D)
60. ● (B) (C) (D)
61. ● (B) (C) (D)
62. (A) ● (C) (D)
63. (A) ● (C) (D)
64. ● (B) (C) (D)
65. ● (B) (C) (D)
66. (A) ● (C) (D)
67. (A) ● (C) (D)
68. (A) (B) ● (D)
69. (A) ● (C) (D)
70. (A) (B) ● (D)
71. (A) (B) ● (D)
72. (A) (B) ● (D)
73. ● (B) (C) (D)
74. (A) (B) ● (D)
75. (A) (B) (C) ●

76. (A) ● (C) (D)
77. (A) (B) (C) ●
78. (A) ● (C) (D)
79. (A) ● (C) (D)
80. ● (B) (C) (D)
81. ● (B) (C) (D)
82. (A) (B) ● (D)
83. (A) (B) ● (D)
84. (A) (B) (C) ●
85. (A) ● (C) (D)

1.   The answer is B.

Proctor testing measures the optimal density of a specific sample of soil. The level of moisture in the sample is a factor in determining the ideal density. The soil is then compacted to within a specific percentage of the Proctor density as specified by the soils engineer so that the soil has the bearing capacity necessary to support the building load.

Soil composition is analyzed through a combination of visual inspection of excavated pits and/or through test borings and laboratory testing of soil samples.

A *percolation* (or "perc") *test* measures the ability of saturated soil to absorb a given quantity of water within a specified period of time. It is used as a factor in septic system design.

Bearing capacity is evaluated by a soils engineer based upon the results of soil composition tests and observations.

2.   The answer is B and D.

Gravel and sand are coarse-grained materials that support building foundations well. Because they have a rough shape, the particles compact tightly and "grip" each other to resist movement. They drain well and are considered very stable soils. Only bedrock surpasses them as a support for a building foundation.

Clay and silt, on the other hand, are not stable. Clay is made up of smooth, disk-shaped particles that slip against each other and are greatly affected by moisture content. Clay shrinks when dry and expands when wet and therefore is not considered a suitable material for foundation support. Silt is stable when dry or damp but unstable when wet. It swells and heaves when frozen and compresses under load. Clay and silt must be removed through excavation or mixed with other materials to form "engineered fill," or building footings constructed on the site must be placed below the unstable stratum on soil that is capable of carrying the load.

Organic soils, such as peat and topsoil, consist of decomposed or decaying plant and animal remains. They are not considered stable soils. Topsoil is rich in nutrients and should be removed from the building site and stockpiled so that it can be redistributed when construction operations have ended and landscaping begins.

3.   The answer is B.

Footings must always be placed at least 1 ft (305) below the frost line to avoid heaving that may occur as the ground freezes and thaws.

Footings must always be placed on soil capable of carrying the weight of the building, but they need not be placed on bedrock; many other soil types can adequately carry the load. Building below the water table is very costly because the site must be dewatered, and should be avoided when possible. It is not necessary to place all footings at the same depth throughout the building. For example, footings may be placed at varying depths because soil properties differ across the site or because the building is to be constructed on a slope.

4.   The answer is B.

The ground meeting a building's foundation should slope away from the building a minimum of $^1/_4$ in/ft (20 mm/m).

5.   The answer is A.

Friction piles are a good choice in the situation described. As the pile is driven into the soil, frictional forces will develop between the soil and the pile, which allow the pile to develop load-carrying capacity even though the end of the pile will not bear on soil capable of carrying the building load.

The bearing stratum is too deep at 100 ft (30 m) for end-bearing piles or belled caissons to be a reasonable or economical choice. The high water table, at 10 ft (3 m) below grade, would make footings and concrete masonry unit foundation walls very expensive when dewatering and waterproofing are added into the project costs.

6.   The answer is C.

Underpinning is the process of strengthening an existing building's foundation. It can be accomplished in a variety of ways depending on the type of existing foundation and how much reinforcement is necessary. It may become necessary to underpin a foundation if adjacent new construction compromises the stability of the existing building's foundation, if major plumbing leaks or flooding saturates the soil and causes it to become unstable, if the subsurface soil has "shrink/swell" tendencies, or if a desired change in building use will result in greater building loads.

Underpinning is accomplished most often with the help of needle beams. The area around the foundation is excavated and a hole is cut into the foundation wall. A needle beam is slipped through the hole and jacked to temporarily support the foundation. A new foundation wall, piles, or caissons capable of carrying the new load or reaching an appropriate bearing stratum are erected underneath the foundation. When complete, the temporary bracing is removed and the foundation is backfilled.

7.   **The answer is C.**

Aggregate shall not be larger than one-third of the slab thickness or three-quarters of the minimum space between reinforcing bars, whichever is smaller.

In U.S. units:

The slab thickness is 6 in, and one-third of this is 2 in.

The rebar is spaced 4 in apart. Number 4 rebar is $1/2$ in in diameter, so the minimum space between reinforcing bars is 4 in + $1/2$ in = $3^1/2$ in. Three-quarters of this is

$$(3.5 \text{ in})(0.75) = 2.625 \text{ in} \quad (2\tfrac{5}{8} \text{ in})$$

The aggregate must not be larger than the smaller of the two values, which is 2 in.

In SI units:

The slab thickness is 150 mm, and one-third of this is 50 mm.

The rebar is spaced 100 mm apart. Number 4 rebar is 13 mm in diameter, so the minimum space between reinforcing bars is 100 mm − 13 mm = 87 mm. Three-quarters of this is

$$(87 \text{ mm})(0.75) = 65.25 \text{ mm}$$

The aggregate must not be larger than the smaller of the two values, which is 50 mm.

8.   **The answer is C.**

Formwork should be constructed first (II), and then a release agent such as oil is applied (I) to make it easier to remove the forms from the cured concrete. It is important to apply the release agent before placing the reinforcing, because if oil is on the surface of the rebar it could prevent the concrete from adhering properly to the steel. Next, the reinforcing bars are placed and tied (IV). When the concrete arrives on site, slump testing is performed (V) to ensure that the mix complies with specified limits for workability and water content. If the results of the slump test are within acceptable limits, the concrete may be poured and vibrated to fill the forms (III).

9.   **The answer is C.**

Water and portland cement chemically react in a process known as *hydration*. Portland cement is a manufactured material that replicates some of the properties of *pozzolana*. The ancient Romans discovered that this type of volcanic ash reacted chemically with water and lime to form an artificial stone.

10.   **The answer is C.**

Epoxy-coated reinforcing bars are used when the concrete will be exposed to chlorides (salts) such as deicing salts and those in seawater. The epoxy coating helps keep the salts from corroding the steel by chemical reaction. An interior column is unlikely to be in contact with chlorides, so it is not necessary to specify epoxy-coated rebar in this application.

11.   **The answer is B.**

A U.S. modular brick is $7^5/8$ in (194) long, $3^5/8$ in (92) thick, and $2^1/4$ in (57) high. The units are sized so that three brick courses plus three $3/8$ in (10) mortar joints are equal to 8 in (203), and the length of a brick plus one $3/8$ in (10) mortar joint also equals 8 in (203).

The dimensions given in option A are those of utility brick, option C lists the dimensions of engineer modular brick, and option D gives the dimensions of a Norman brick.

For more information on brick sizing, coursing, and position, see *Technical Notes 10: Dimensioning and Estimating Brick Masonry*, published by the Brick Industry Association, at www.gobrick.org.

12.   **The answer is D.**

Chairs are small wire supports that help to keep rebar a specified distance from the outside of the concrete and help ensure adequate concrete cover. A *bolster* is a type of chair used in broad slabs or beams.

13.   **The answer is B.**

For slip resistance, a *broom finish* (achieved by passing an industrial broom in parallel strokes across the surface of the uncured concrete) is the best choice.

A *float finish* is a rough finish intended for outdoor surfaces and interior slabs that will become the substrate for a finish material that does not require a perfectly smooth underlayment, such as carpet or tile. The *troweled finishes* (hard steel-troweled and light steel-troweled) are very smooth and can be sealed or painted to become the final floor finish, or they can become the substrate for a finish material that requires a perfectly smooth surface, such as vinyl composition tile.

14. The answer is D.

An *isolation joint* allows two sections of a building to move independently, and is typically used where an addition meets an existing building or where two different materials meet. It is also called an *abutment joint*.

A *control joint* is a groove or saw cut that provides an area of weakness so that expected cracking caused by expansion and contraction can be limited to a predetermined area. A *construction joint* is a break between two successive concrete pours; the concrete is generally keyed at this location and reinforcing that is incorporated into the first pour should extend into the second. *Expansion joints* allow for the natural movement of a building due to expansion and contraction. Expansion joints must be covered with a watertight barrier and are located at regular intervals in long expanses of masonry or concrete, where taller building forms meet shorter ones, at corners, and at openings.

15. The answer is A.

Type M mortar should be specified for exterior applications at or below grade.

Type N or S is best for exterior applications above grade and for interior load-bearing walls. Type O is well suited for interior and protected exterior non-load-bearing partitions.

16. The answer is D.

SW, or "severe weathering," is highly resistant to freeze/thaw cycles and is suitable for use in harsh climates. MW stands for "moderate weathering," and NW represents "negligible or no weathering." FW is not a grading for brick.

17. The answer is D.

Raked joints are not recommended for exterior use because water can pool in the tiny void between bricks, seep into the pores of the materials, and eventually damage the masonry and mortar. Concave, flush, and vee joints are all acceptable for exterior applications. The concave and vee joints are tooled joints that slope or curve toward the ground and shed water from the joint. The flush joint is struck flush to the face of the brick, so there is no space for water to accumulate. Another acceptable joint for exterior use is the weathered (or weather-struck) joint, which also slopes downward to encourage water to drain from the crevice.

18. The answer is D.

Weep holes should be located at any location where water may accumulate within a multi-wythe, cavity, or veneer wall. The weep holes allow the water to drain or be wicked out of the wall cavity. Water tends to accumulate at the bottom of a wall or where any penetration through the wall creates a "shelf," such as above a window or at a steel angle. Both flashing and weep holes at 24 in (610) on center, minimum, should be provided at each of the locations listed.

Weep holes are formed by placing short pieces of rope or plastic units in the mortar joint as it is being laid. The spacer is then removed after the mortar hardens, leaving a small hole. Alternatively, some masons choose to simply leave a portion of the bed joint unmortared. Either way, the opening gives water a way to escape from the wall assembly and helps to prevent condensation from accumulating within.

19. The answer is C.

The least destructive technique should always be recommended when dealing with historic buildings and fragile old building materials. Hand washing with water and a stiff brush is the gentlest cleaning method and will probably remove most of the dirt from the surface of the brick. Missing or deteriorating mortar should be removed and replaced with compatible mortar, and the mortar should be restruck to shed water from the joints. This process is called *repointing* or *tuck pointing*.

Pressure washing (sometimes called power washing) can leave water marks on soft brick and can dislodge crumbling mortar, creating openings and allowing water to be forced inside the wall cavity. Adding an acidic ingredient to the washing solution may cause additional damage to the brick. Sandblasting will likely destroy soft brick and mortar.

20. The answer is B.

Limestone is a type of *sedimentary* rock formed through the action of water and wind and comprised of elements left behind from the skeletons of marine organisms. Other examples of sedimentary rock used as building materials are brownstone and sandstone.

Igneous rock was deposited while molten; a common example is granite. *Metamorphic* rock is either sedimentary or igneous rock that has been transformed by heat and pressure. Examples are marble, soapstone, and slate. Monumental is not a type of rock.

21.   **The answer is B.**

32/16 is the *span rating* for the plywood sheathing. This designation means that the material has been tested according to the standards of the Engineered Wood Association and can be used to span rafters 32 in on center or joists 16 in on center.

The span rating and other information about the material can be found stamped on each sheet of plywood. The following illustration shows an APA stamp.

Used with permission from APA— The Engineered Wood Association.

22.   **The answer is D.**

Mortise locks are the most secure type of lockset because the mechanism is concealed within the leaf of the door.

Unit locks are installed into a notch cut into the leaf of the door. *Cylinder locks* are installed through a hole drilled in the leaf. *Rim locks* are mounted on the face of the leaf. Because each of these types of locksets leaves portions of the mechanism exposed, they can be more easily tampered with and are not as secure as the mortise lockset.

23.   **The answer is C.**

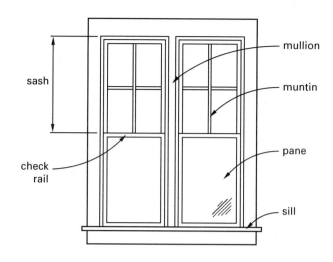

24.   **The answer is B.**

The *equivalent thickness* is a measurement of the amount of concrete in a hollow core block. It is equal to the thickness that the block would be if it were the same height and length but were cast without holes. This information is often necessary for calculating fire resistance of assemblies.

A nominal 12 in (305) concrete block is actually $11^5/8$ in (295) thick. Multiply the actual thickness by the percentage of solids to arrive at equivalent thickness. The equivalent thickness of this block is 75% of $11^5/8$ in (295), or $8^3/4$ in (222).

25.   **The answer is C.**

Skewback is the horizontal distance from the upper corner of the masonry opening to the upper outside corner of the jack arch. It is equivalent to $^1/2$ in per foot (42 mm per meter) of span (that is, $^1/{24}$ the length of the span) for each 4 in (102) of arch depth.

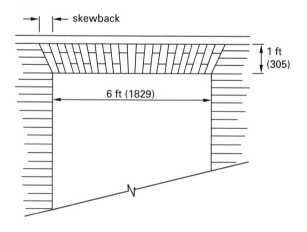

In U.S. units:

$$\text{skewback} = \left(\frac{\text{span}}{24}\right)\left(\frac{\text{arch depth}}{4 \text{ in}}\right)$$

$$= \left(\frac{(6 \text{ ft})\left(12 \frac{\text{in}}{\text{ft}}\right)}{24}\right)\left(\frac{12 \text{ in}}{4 \text{ in}}\right)$$

$$= 9 \text{ in}$$

In SI units:

$$\text{skewback} = \left(\frac{\text{span}}{24}\right)\left(\frac{\text{arch depth}}{102 \text{ mm}}\right)$$

$$= \left(\frac{1829 \text{ mm}}{24}\right)\left(\frac{305 \text{ mm}}{102 \text{ mm}}\right)$$

$$= 228 \text{ mm}$$

26.   **The answer is B.**

Life-cycle cost is an analysis of how much it costs to install and maintain a given material over a given period of time.

First, calculate the installation cost for each material by multiplying the quantity of material by the cost per unit. Next, calculate the future costs of replacement or refinishing at the 10-year and 20-year points using the same formula and the projected costs. Finally, add the initial, 10-year, and 20-year values to determine the total life-cycle cost.

In U.S. units:

For plastic laminate countertops, the installation cost is

$$(8 \text{ linear ft})\left(\frac{\$60}{\text{linear ft}}\right) = \$480$$

10-year replacement would cost

$$(8 \text{ linear ft})\left(\frac{\$70}{\text{linear ft}}\right) = \$560$$

20-year replacement would cost

$$(8 \text{ linear ft})\left(\frac{\$80}{\text{linear ft}}\right) = \$640$$

The Life-cycle cost is

$$\$480 + \$560 + \$640 = \$1680$$

For solid-surface countertops, the installation cost is

$$(8 \text{ linear ft})\left(\frac{\$110}{\text{linear ft}}\right) = \$880$$

10-year refinishing would cost

$$(8 \text{ linear ft})\left(\frac{\$10}{\text{linear ft}}\right) = \$80$$

20-year refinishing would cost

$$(8 \text{ linear ft})\left(\frac{\$20}{\text{linear ft}}\right) = \$160$$

The Life-cycle cost is

$$\$880 + \$80 + \$160 = \$1120$$

In SI units:

For plastic laminate countertops, the installation cost is

$$(2 \text{ m})\left(\frac{\$200}{\text{m}}\right) = \$400$$

10-year replacement would cost

$$(2 \text{ m})\left(\frac{\$240}{\text{m}}\right) = \$480$$

20-year replacement would cost

$$(2 \text{ m})\left(\frac{\$270}{\text{m}}\right) = \$540$$

The Life-cycle cost is

$$\$400 + \$480 + \$540 = \$1420$$

For solid-surface countertops, the installation cost is

$$(2 \text{ m})\left(\frac{\$370}{\text{m}}\right) = \$740$$

10-year refinishing would cost

$$(2 \text{ m})\left(\frac{\$30}{\text{m}}\right) = \$60$$

20-year refinishing would cost

$$(2 \text{ m})\left(\frac{\$60}{\text{m}}\right) = \$120$$

The Life-cycle cost is

$$\$740 + \$60 + \$120 = \$920$$

Although the initial installation cost of the solid-surface material is almost twice that of the plastic laminate, the life-cycle cost of the solid surface is much lower.

27.　The answer is C.

This symbol represents a double-fillet weld. The arrow would point to the location of the weld. The triangle is the symbol for a fillet weld; two indicate a double-fillet weld. Symbols below the horizontal line refer to welds on the arrow side; symbols above the line refer to welds on the other side.

The American Institute of Steel Construction's *Steel Construction Manual* features a full explanation of basic and supplementary weld symbols and instructions for using this symbol system to explain what type of weld is required.

28.　The answer is A.

The *Steiner tunnel test* is not a concrete test. It is used to determine the surface burning characteristics of interior finish materials.

The cylinder, electrical impedance, and Kelly ball tests all quantify different characteristics of concrete. The *cylinder test* involves breaking a cylinder formed of concrete from a specific pour in order to test the concrete's compressive strength during the curing process. The *electrical impedance test* determines the moisture level of a slab by measuring the amount of electricity conducted through the material. Slabs with a greater moisture content conduct more electricity. The *Kelly ball test* measures the consistency of the uncured concrete. A metal ball is dropped into freshly laid concrete, and the depression caused by the ball is measured and compared to the slump test results.

29.　The answer is B, C, and D.

By definition, the *means of egress* consists of the exit access, the exit, and the exit discharge.

The means of egress must lead to a public way, but the public way is not part of the means of egress. The common path of travel (or common path of egress travel) is that portion of exit access that the occupants are required to traverse before two separate and distinct paths of egress travel to two exits are available. Although an important feature, this is not a part of the means of egress. The travel distance is the distance from any point in the exit access to the nearest exit.

30.　The answer is 4.

Normal-slope asphalt or fiberglass shingles are to be installed on roofs with a pitch of 4:12 or greater. The two materials are similar in appearance and installation method, but fiberglass shingles offer better fire resistance. In most cases, the manufacturer will not honor the warranty if normal-slope products are placed on a low-slope roof. Low-slope asphalt and fiberglass shingles are available for roof pitches of 3:12 to 4:12 and require a different underlayment than the normal-slope products.

Better choices for low-slope roofing materials are welded or soldered metal, rolled asphalt, or membrane roofing.

31.　The answer is A.

Vapor retarders (which are sometimes called *vapor barriers*) are always installed on the "warm" side of a wall, usually between the stud and the interior finish material. The vapor retarder can be made of foil, plastic, or paper and should be applied with no breaks. All seams should be lapped for maximum effectiveness. For this reason, in cold climates it can be preferable to specify unfaced batt insulation and a separate vapor retarder.

If vapor retarders are incorrectly placed on the "cool" side (the exterior of the stud), condensation will develop within the wall cavity, which may lead to decay or mold problems.

32.　The answer is A and D.

The structural slab is a consideration only as part of the entire floor/ceiling assembly. Neither thermal insulation nor sound absorption is a consideration in a ceiling's fire resistance. Style is not as important as whether or not the grid is rated.

33.　The answer is C.

Wood flooring installed over a slab on grade should be placed on treated wood sleepers that are set in a layer of mastic. Sleepers are generally 2×4s laid flat at 16 in (406) on center. A layer of polyethylene vapor barrier should be placed over the sleepers but under the finish flooring material.

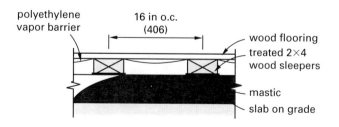

34.   The answer is 3.3.

R-value is a measure of resistance to heat flow. All building materials have *R*-values, but the term is most often used when discussing insulation, because to meet the minimum *R*-values required by building and energy codes, an assembly must almost always include some type of insulating material. Fiberglass batt insulation is a common choice for a wood or light-gauge steel-framed wall assembly. Each inch of fiberglass batt insulation has an *R*-value of 3.3. The batt insulation installed in a typical 2×4 stud wall offers an *R*-value of approximately 12. By increasing the size of the studs used for framing the exterior walls to 2×6, the *R*-value of the insulation may be increased to 19.

35.   The answer is B.

Spruce trees are not inherently resistant to decay, but the heartwood of cedar, redwood, and cypress all possess a natural resistance that makes them a good choice for use in exterior applications such as siding, shingles or shakes, and decking. The outer rings of these species do not possess the same decay-resistant qualities, so it is important to specify that only heartwood may be used when decay resistance is of concern. These woods are considerably more expensive than other species that are more commonly used for construction such as pine, hemlock, fir, and spruce.

Species that are not inherently decay resistant must be chemically treated to protect them from rotting when exposed to moisture. Waterborne salts are pressure-impregnated into the wood to prevent decay, often for as long as 30 years. After a waiting period, salt-treated wood can be painted or stained.

36.   The answer is C.

Stainless steel would be the least desirable choice for flashing material when used near an aluminum window assembly because of the metals listed, it is furthest from aluminum on the galvanic action table, even further than copper. The more dissimilar the materials, the more current will flow between the two and speed corrosion. This process is called *electrolysis.*

The best choice would be to use aluminum flashing and aluminum fasteners and accessories. However, aluminum can also react with alkaline materials, so it must be protected from mortar and concrete. Nonreactive materials such as plastics are also an option, but they should be carefully researched, as plastics tend to degrade more quickly than metals. Any dissimilar materials in proximity to one another must always be carefully separated with a layer of nonreactive material such as rubber or neoprene.

37.   The answer is C.

The Reliance Building, built in Chicago in 1894 through 1895, was one of the first buildings to use an all-steel frame and exploit the possibilities of the curtain-wall construction technique. Its steel grid is concealed behind tile ornamentation, but the pattern of the framing members is expressed in the exterior skin. The thin structural members and lightness of the building is a sharp contrast to the firm's work just five years prior at the Monadnock Building, described in option A.

Credit for the first curtain-wall structure, option B, is given to William LeBaron Jenney's Home Insurance Building, which was built in Chicago a decade before the Reliance Building. However, Jenney's building used a curtain wall on just the upper stories. Louis Sullivan's Carson Pirie Scott Department Store (also known as the Schlesenger & Meyer Store and built in 1899 through 1904) in Chicago features highly detailed cast-iron ornament with organic motifs on the street level and a Chicago-style fenestration above.

38.   The answer is C.

Louis I. Kahn is best known for his work with heavy masses of masonry and concrete juxtaposed against openings that admit ever-changing daylight into the interior spaces of the buildings. The designs of buildings such as the Richards Medical Research Building at the University of Pennsylvania (1957 through 1961) and the Salk Institute in La Jolla, California (1959 through 1965), are both driven by Kahn's fascination with natural light.

Ludwig Mies van der Rohe employed steel and glass in the majority of his structures and was known for expressing the structural framework on the facade of a building. Examples of his work include the Seagram Building in New York City (1954 through 1958) and the Farnsworth House in Illinois (1945 through 1951).

Le Corbusier "sculpted" his buildings with reinforced concrete. His design often employed *pilotis* (reinforced concrete columns) and sharp planes of pure white concrete. His work at the Villa Savoye in France (1928 through 1929) and his writings in *Towards a New Architecture* best illustrate his design philosophy.

In his later work, Frank Lloyd Wright often used reinforced concrete, but in a much more sculptural and organic way than Le Corbusier. At Fallingwater in western Pennsylvania (1937) and the Guggenheim Museum in New York City (1956 through 1959), Wright exploited the properties of reinforced concrete to create cantilevered and curved forms with rounded edges, giving the material a curved, softer edge.

39.   The answer is D.

In *rift sawing*, boards are cut radially from the center of the log. This produces a very straight and consistent vertical grain, and this type of cut is typically only used for sawing oak. However, the log must be repositioned for each cut, so the process is very labor intensive. Also, because the boards are not cut perpendicular to one another, there is a great deal of waste in rift sawing. For these reasons, it is the most expensive sawing technique.

Quartersawing involves dividing a log into quarters and then cutting boards perpendicular to the grain. Like rift sawing, it produces boards with straight grain running parallel to the length of the board. However, the grain is not as straight with quartersawing as it would be with rift sawing.

Plain sawing and *flat sawing* are the same thing. The boards are cut in straight lines across the grain of the log. The grain tends to be more uneven than quartersawn or rift-sawn boards, but it is this technique that produces the "curvy" grain often seen on framing members. Boards cut from the periphery of the log tend to cup or warp a little more than quarter- or rift-sawn boards because of the curve of the grain.

40.   The answer is A.

Flush construction is typically the most expensive because the face of the door or drawer lies flush with the face frame of the cabinet. This construction technique leaves little room for error because everything must align perfectly.

Each of the other construction techniques (*flush overlay*, *reveal overlay*, and *lipped overlay*) have doors or drawers whose faces overlap the cabinet's face frame.

Additional information on grades of cabinetry and types of cabinetry construction can be found in the Architectural Woodwork Institute's *Architectural Woodwork Quality Standards.*

41.   The answer is C.

Waterproofing membranes—usually building felt saturated with bituminous material, sheet plastics, or thin sheets of bentonite clay—can be easily punctured when the foundation is backfilled. As their effectiveness is entirely dependent on their watertightness, it is prudent to provide a protection board to prevent rocks or machinery from damaging the surface.

Dampproofing controls moisture that is not under hydrostatic pressure, while *waterproofing* is required to control moisture that is affected by hydrostatic pressure. Waterproofing

techniques are generally more costly and difficult to apply. Membrane coatings are an excellent choice for waterproofing but are not generally required for dampproofing. In a situation where waterproofing is required, hydrostatic pressure against the wall can be lessened by providing geotextile matting ("filter fabric") and a foundation drain set in gravel at the footing.

42.   The answer is D.

A standard roll-in-type shower is required by the *ADA/ABA Guidelines* to be at least 60 in (1525) wide by 30 in (760) deep, as shown. In addition, a clear floor space of 60 in (1525) by 30 in (760) must be provided adjacent to the opening of the shower enclosure. The total floor area that must be allocated for both the shower and the required clear floor space is 60 in (1525) by 60 in (1525).

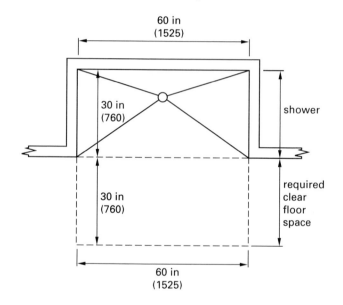

43.   The answer is B.

Although options A, B, and C are all valid approaches to reducing the sound transmission from one space to another and option D is a good approach for increasing the absorption of sound within an office, the most critical strategy to employ is to extend the partition walls from floor deck to floor deck and seal the connections well (option B). Any gaps, such as a partition that only extends a few inches above a suspended ceiling, will allow sound to pass freely from the office to the corridor and vice versa.

44.   The answer is D.

When preparing door and hardware schedules, it is important to note the *hand* of the door. Referring to the hand is a standard method of describing the location of the hinges and which way the door swings. If a person standing on the outside of a door cannot see the hinges and the door swings away, it is either right hand (RH) or left hand (LH), depending upon which side the hinges are located. If the door swings toward the person, it is either right hand reverse (RHR) or left hand reverse (LHR), again depending upon the location of the hinges.

45. The answer is D.

The 2-hour rated wall assembly consists of 2×4 studs placed at 16 in (406) on center, with two layers of ⅝ in (16) type X (fire-rated) gypsum board attached to each side of the wall.

All of the other wall sections depict 1-hour rated assemblies.

46. The answer is A.

Rapidly renewable building materials are made from plants that can be grown and harvested relatively quickly, generally within 10 years. Wheat board cabinetry, linoleum (which is made from jute, linseed oil, and other natural and sustainable materials), and bamboo paneling are considered rapidly renewable resources.

Flooring manufactured from reclaimed barn beams would be considered a "green" building material but not a rapidly renewable one. Recovering the beams and sawing them into flooring allows the material to be reused for a new purpose and prevents the harvesting of other hardwoods that are not rapidly renewable.

47. The answer is B.

The dimensions given in option B are the correct dimensions for a toilet-stall configuration according to *ADA/ABA Guidelines.*

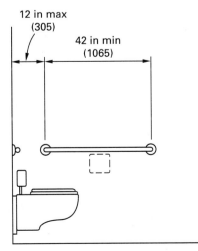

48. The answer is B.

Placing the studs at 12 in (305) on center rather than at the typical 16 in (406) spacing would increase the load-carrying capacity of a stud wall, but would not give lateral stability.

Diagonal bracing, sheathing, and steel rods with turnbuckles placed on the diagonal between the framing members are all methods of adding lateral stability to the structure of a building.

49. The answer is C.

The structural shape shown is an S shape, which is also known as an American Standard beam. S shapes are very similar to W shapes, but the flanges of an S shape are tapered rather than straight and are typically narrower.

A full description and diagrams of each of the structural steel shapes can be found in the American Institute of Steel Construction's *Steel Construction Manual.*

50. The answer is B, C, and D.

Stainless steel can be welded, is much stronger than bronze, and is highly resistant to corrosion. It is primarily an alloy of steel and chromium, but sometimes nickel and/or other elements are added.

51. The answer is B.

According to the *International Building Code*, the minimum depth (x) required for a hearth is 16 in (406) from the face of the fireplace. However, if the fireplace opening is 6 ft² (0.56 m²) or greater, the requirement is increased to 20 in (508). The opening of the fireplace shown is 3 ft × 2 ft (0.91 m × 0.61 m) or 6 ft² (0.56 m²).

In U.S. units:

The hearth must extend at least 8 in on either side of the fireplace opening, so the width of the hearth must be

$$36 \text{ in} + 8 \text{ in} + 8 \text{ in} = 52 \text{ in}$$

In SI units:

The hearth must extend at least 203 mm on either side of the fireplace opening, so the width of the hearth must be

$$914 \text{ mm} + 203 \text{ mm} + 203 \text{ mm} = 1320 \text{ mm}$$

52. The answer is A.

Stretcher bricks have their faces on the exterior of the wall oriented horizontally. This is the most common position, such as in a running or stacked bond wall.

Soldier bricks have their faces exterior and oriented vertically. Soldier courses are often used as an accent, to delineate a floor line on the exterior of the building, or above a window opening.

Rowlock bricks have their ends exterior and oriented vertically. They are often used as an accent or as a window sill.

Sailor bricks have their beds exterior and of the brick oriented vertically. They are used primarily as an accent.

Although not pictured, *shiner* bricks have their beds exterior and oriented horizontally, and *header* bricks have their ends exterior and oriented horizontally.

53. The answer is B.

A *flitch beam* combines wood and steel into one member with load-carrying capacity far exceeding that of wood alone. Flitch beams are sometimes referred to as *sandwich beams*.

54. The answer is D.

Windows are rarely reused in sustainable design projects that convert old buildings to a new use. Old windows do not possess the energy efficiency of a new window that could be installed in the existing masonry opening. The exterior building envelope and structural framing of an old building is often intact and can be reused without diminishing the building's energy efficiency.

Another material that is almost always replaced in a green building reuse project is the nonstructural roofing material (membrane roofing, shingles, etc.). Again, newer materials far surpass the older, existing materials in terms of building energy efficiency.

For purposes of LEED credit assessment, windows and nonstructural roofing material are always deducted from the existing building and shell reuse calculations.

55. The answer is C.

Beams are defined as wood members that are at least 5 in (127) wide with a depth at least 2 in (51) greater than their width.

Boards are pieces of wood smaller than 2 in (51) thick and 2 in (51) wide. Dimensional lumber is 2 in (51) to 4 in (102) thick and 2 in (51) or more wide.

Posts and timbers are at least 5 in (127) wide and at least 5 in (127) deep, but not more than 2 in (51) deeper than the width.

56. The answer is B.

The amount of *embodied energy* in a building material is a measure of the resources that went into its acquisition (mining, harvesting, etc.), processing (transportation, the mechanical processes necessary to convert the material from one form to another, etc.), and final production and delivery (packaging, transportation, etc.).

57. The answer is A.

A *cricket* is a small gable placed directly behind a chimney to direct water away from the masonry and encourage it to drain from the roof rather than allowing it to accumulate behind the chimney.

58. The answer is A, B, E, and F.

Laminated glass is good for acoustical control because of its mass and the damping quality of the plastic interlayer. Laminated glass can be used for decorative purposes by using a decorative interlayer between the sheets of glass. It is also considered to be safety glazing and provides excellent resistance to breaking, as a security measure. With the correct thickness and types of interlayers, laminated glass can also provide bullet resistance.

Although some laminated glass can carry a 30-minute fire rating, fire protection is not a common use of this material. The insulation value of laminated glass is negligible unless the glass is used with other glazing in an insulated glass unit.

59. The answer is B.

Auguste Perret, a French architect practicing in the early 1900s, designed most of his buildings using a revolutionary new material: reinforced concrete. His best-known work, Notre Dame du Raincy in Paris (1922) used "ferroconcrete" in ways that it had never been used before: as tall, slender columns and vaulted ceilings all accented by detailed tracery windows. Although the forms employed had historical precedents, the technology behind the design was thoroughly modern.

Perret is also notable in architectural history as a teacher and early employer of one of the masters of reinforced concrete design, Le Corbusier. According to legend, Le Corbusier and Perret often butted heads, as the apprentice felt Perret was too tied to traditional forms and ornament.

60. The answer is A.

Concrete gains the most compressive strength during the first few days of curing. This is the most critical time in the curing process, and it is important that the concrete be protected from freezing or evaporation during this time. If the concrete is unprotected and environmental conditions are unfavorable, the ultimate compressive strength of the concrete could be greatly reduced.

Theoretically, concrete continues to gain strength well after the 28th day. But for the purposes of design strengths and testing, the compressive strength of concrete is always referred to as its strength 28 days after it is placed.

61. The answer is A.

Asphalt, which is dark to black in color, has the lowest albedo of the paving materials listed. *Albedo* is a measurement of the material's solar reflectance: the higher the number, the more reflective the surface.

Dark paving materials retain more heat than light-colored materials, so those portions of the site heat up faster, artificially elevating the temperature of the entire area. The worst offenders are new blacktop parking lots; fresh asphalt has an albedo of 0.05 to 0.10.

Heat islands are portions of a site or region that are warmer than adjacent undeveloped areas. To reduce heat islands, the most desirable paving materials are those with the highest albedo, such as concrete made with white cement, which has an albedo of 0.70 to 0.80 when new.

62. The answer is B.

Steel reinforcing bars are most often spliced by overlapping the two bars a specified distance, sometimes expressed in terms of a number of bar widths or diameters. There are two types of lap splices: *contact splices*, where the bars are wired together, and *non-contact splices*, where the bars are laid in parallel and overlapped the specified distanced but are not fastened to one another.

Mechanical splices use a connection piece to link the bars end to end. Metal sleeves and cylinder connectors are two examples of devices that may be used to form a mechanical splice. Mechanical splices can be classified as tension only,

compression only, or tension-compression, depending on which stresses the connector is designed to resist.

Welded connections, while possible, are not recommended.

More information about steel reinforcing for concrete can be found at the Concrete Reinforcing Steel Institute's website, www.crsi.org.

63. The answer is B.

A *cant strip* is an angled piece of wood blocking that eases the transition between the roof deck and the parapet wall when installing a roofing system so that the membranes or roofing felts do not crack or split when they are applied. Rather than bending them at a 90° angle, the cant strip allows the transition to be made with two 45° angles and minimizes the likelihood of damage from cracking or splitting. In addition, the slope helps the water to drain away from the joint and allows the flashing and membranes to be lapped in a way that keeps water from entering.

64. The answer is A.

ACQ (which stands for *alkaline copper quat*) is a wood preservative that contains up to 96% copper. It has taken the place of CCA (chromated copper arsenate), which was formerly used for pressure-treated lumber until it was banned for residential use by the Environmental Protection Agency because of concern about its arsenic content.

Any metals used in proximity to ACQ-treated wood must be compatible with copper according to the galvanic series. Aluminum flashing or connectors should never be used with treated lumber. Copper is the best choice, but while copper flashing is widely available, not all necessary fasteners are manufactured in copper. Other acceptable choices are stainless steel and hot-dip galvanized products.

65. The answer is A.

Triglyphs and metopes are parts of the frieze in the Doric order. A *triglyph* looks like a raised rectangular plaque applied to the horizontal frieze band. It is carved with flutes so that the raised, flat part of the plaque looks similar to Roman numeral III (hence, *triglyph*). *Metopes* are the nearly square, recessed areas in between the triglyphs. Sometimes they were left unadorned, but often an ornament was carved within this area. The Parthenon is a good example of a structure with very clearly defined triglyphs and ornamented metopes.

66.   The answer is B.

In cold, snowy climates, ice dams can be a major problem. The warmth of the attic space below heats up the roof and causes the snow that has accumulated on the roof to melt. The eaves are not as warm as the rest of the roof, so the melting snow and water runs down the roof toward the gutters but refreezes when it comes in contact with the cold eaves. The ice forms a dam, trapping more water behind it, which either freezes and becomes part of the dam or makes its way down through the walls and can cause leaks or mold.

The best strategy is the keep the attic and roof as cold as possible. Providing ridge and soffit vents helps the cold exterior air to flow through the space and regulate the temperature. Properly sealing and insulating any ductwork in the attic keeps heat from escaping and warming the attic space, and caulking all penetrations keeps warm air from the occupied spaces from creeping into the attic.

Simply installing additional batt insulation between the roof rafters (without providing an airspace between the roof sheathing and the insulation) will make the problem worse. Instead, additional insulation should be added on the attic floor to keep the warmth within the occupied spaces and the attic and roof very cold.

67.   The answer is B.

Information provided in resources such as the series of publications from R.S. Means provides valuable information about construction costs, including labor, materials, and how these costs compare in different regions of the country. Location factors can very greatly depending on the local economy, prevailing wage rates, difficulty of transporting materials to the site, demand for construction services, and numerous other factors.

Begin by increasing the $300,000 original construction cost to today's dollars using the inflation rate given, 2%, for three years.

$$C_{today} = C_{3\,yr\,ago}(1 + i)^n = (\$300,000)(1.02)^3$$

$$= \$318,362.40$$

It would cost about $318,362 to build the same building in Pittsburgh today.

Next, calculate the cost of construction in Durham. The ratio of the construction costs in the two cities is equivalent to the ratio of their location factors.

$$\frac{C_{Pittsburgh}}{C_{Durham}} = \frac{f_{Pittsburgh}}{f_{Durham}}$$

$$C_{Durham} = \left(\frac{f_{Durham}}{f_{Pittsburgh}}\right)C_{Pittsburgh}$$

$$= \left(\frac{75}{100}\right)(\$318,362)$$

$$= \$238,771.50$$

It can be estimated that it will cost about $238,772 to build the same building in Durham, North Carolina, today.

68.   The answer is C.

Polyisocyanurate is a type of roof insulation and can be found in Division 07—Thermal and Moisture Protection.

The CSI (which stands for Construction Specifications Institute) divisions are a system used for cataloguing information about building materials and equipment and for organizing specifications. *Sweets Catalog* and most firms' product libraries are arranged according to this system. Traditionally, there were 16 CSI divisions, and within the divisions, each item was assigned a five-digit code or section number.

In 2004, CSI introduced a 50-category cataloguing system and a six-digit numbering system; this was revised in 2010. The numbering system classifies polyisocyanurate as "07 22 00—Roof and Deck Insulation." Each two-digit level provides additional information about the item, and the expanded system allows more materials and technologies to be classified.

The MasterFormat divisions are as follows.

Procurement & Contracting Requirements Group

> Division 00—Procurement and Contracting Requirements

Specifications Group

> *General Requirements Subgroup*
>
> Division 01—General Requirements
>
> *Facility Construction Subgroup*
>
> Division 02—Existing Conditions
>
> Division 03—Concrete
>
> Division 04—Masonry
>
> Division 05—Metals
>
> Division 06—Wood, Plastics, and Composites
>
> Division 07—Thermal and Moisture Protection
>
> Division 08—Openings
>
> Division 09—Finishes

Division 10—Specialties

Division 11—Equipment

Division 12—Furnishings

Division 13—Special Construction

Division 14—Conveying Equipment

Division 15—Reserved for future expansion

Division 16—Reserved for future expansion

Division 17—Reserved for future expansion

Division 18—Reserved for future expansion

Division 19—Reserved for future expansion

Facility Services Subgroup

Division 20—Reserved for future expansion

Division 21—Fire Suppression

Division 22—Plumbing

Division 23—Heating, Ventilating, and Air Conditioning

Division 24—Reserved for future expansion

Division 25—Integrated Automation

Division 26—Electrical

Division 27—Communications

Division 28—Electronic Safety and Security

Division 29—Reserved for future expansion

Site and Infrastructure Subgroup

Division 30—Reserved for future expansion

Division 31—Earthwork

Division 32—Exterior Improvements

Division 33—Utilities

Division 34—Transportation

Division 35—Waterway and Marine

Division 36—Reserved for future expansion

Division 37—Reserved for future expansion

Division 38—Reserved for future expansion

Division 39—Reserved for future expansion

Process Equipment Subgroup

Division 40—Process Integration

Division 41—Material Processing and Handling Equipment

Division 42—Process Heating, Cooling, and Drying Equipment

Division 43—Process Gas and Liquid Handling, Purification, and Storage Equipment

Division 44—Pollution and Waste Control Equipment

Division 45—Industry-Specific Manufacturing Equipment

Division 46—Water and Wastewater Equipment

Division 47—Reserved for future expansion

Division 48—Electrical Power Generation

Division 49—Reserved for future expansion

As the transition is made from the old system to the new, both ways are likely to be referred to in daily practice and written specifications. Information about the CSI numbering system can be accessed in electronic format on the CSI website, www.csinet.org.

69. The answer is B.

PM, or *polymer-modified*, mineral-based systems have high impact resistance and provide good insulation. They consist of a base and finish coat of synthetic stucco applied over XPS, or *extruded polystyrene*, insulation board.

PB, or *polymer-based*, systems are made up of a very thin base coat of portland cement and polymer over fiberglass mesh with a thin finish coat of polymer-based synthetic stucco over EPS, or *expanded polystyrene*, insulation board. They are lighter in weight than PM systems, but because their plaster coats are so thin, they do not resist impact well.

MB, or *mineral-based*, systems are basically conventional three-coat portland cement stucco systems. They are very impact resistant, but since the stucco is not applied over an insulation board, the system does not offer the insulation of PB and PM systems.

70. The answer is C.

Nine 2×6 studs will be needed for each of the three walls, so 27 studs will be needed in all.

In U.S. units:

Each 2×6 stud will be 8 ft long, and 27 studs are needed, so the total length needed is 27 times 8 ft, or 216 ft.

Board-feet is a measurement that refers to a piece of lumber 1 in thick by 12 in wide by 12 in long, or 144 in^3. A piece of wood 2 in thick by 6 in wide by 12 in long is equivalent to a board-foot. Therefore, the contractor will need to purchase 216 board-feet of lumber to complete the project.

In SI units:

Each 2×6 stud will be 2.44 m long, and 27 studs are needed, so the total length needed is 27 times 2.44 m, or 65.9 m.

Board-feet is a measurement that refers to a piece of lumber 25 mm thick by 305 mm wide by 305 mm long. A 2×6 is about 51 mm thick by 152 mm wide, so a 305 mm length of 2×6 is equivalent to a board foot. The number of 305 mm lengths needed to make 2.44 m is 65,900 mm/305 mm = 216. Therefore, the contractor will need to purchase 216 board-feet of lumber to complete the project.

71.   The answer is C.

The *panel* system would be the least desirable type of curtain-wall system for this building. A panel system is economical and practical only for structures with large numbers of identical panels.

The other three types of systems can be more easily adapted for irregular panel configurations.

72.   The answer is C.

Heavy timber beams were traditionally chamfered to increase their fire resistance. *Chamfering* means carving off an inch of so of wood on the diagonal at each exposed corner of the beam. Thin corners of wood are easily ignited, so removing them through chamfering makes it more difficult for the beam to catch on fire.

73.   The answer is A.

Flat paint finishes contain the greatest amount of pigment relative to the amount of vehicle. *Pigment* is what gives paint its color; vehicle is what makes it stick to the wall.

74.   The answer is C.

A *tolerance* is an amount that an actual dimension can be off from the dimension specified. Tolerances can vary greatly depending on the materials in question. Tolerances are particularly important in stairway design, because as a person moves up or down the steps, he or she expects each step to be the same height and depth as the previous step. If the steps are different, the user may trip and become injured. The height of stair risers and the depth of stair treads are permitted by the IBC to differ by up to 0.375 in (9.5).

75.   The answer is D.

In U.S. units:

The general rule of thumb for choosing an appropriate elevator speed in feet per minute is to multiply the height of the elevator's rise in feet by 1.6 and add 350 ft.

$$S = 1.6r + 350 \text{ ft}$$
$$r = \left(15 \frac{\text{ft}}{\text{story}}\right)(4 \text{ stories}) = 60 \text{ ft}$$
$$S = (1.6)(60 \text{ ft}) + 350 \text{ ft} = 446 \text{ ft}$$

The most appropriate choice is the elevator with a speed of 450 ft/min.

In SI units:

The general rule of thumb for choosing an appropriate elevator speed in meters per minute is to multiply the height of the elevator's rise in meters by 1.6 and add 106.7 m.

$$S = 1.6r + 106.7 \text{ m}$$
$$r = \left(4.6 \frac{\text{m}}{\text{story}}\right)(4 \text{ stories}) = 18.4 \text{ m}$$
$$S = (1.6 \text{ m})(18.4) + 106.7 \text{ m} = 136.1 \text{ m}$$

Converting to meters per second.

$$\left(136.1 \frac{\text{m}}{\text{min}}\right)\left(\frac{1 \text{ min}}{60 \text{ s}}\right) = 2.27 \text{ m/s}$$

The most appropriate choice is the elevator with a speed of 2.3 m/s.

76.   The answer is B.

A 3 ft 6 in (1067) wide center-opening door will allow two people to enter or exit an elevator simultaneously.

77.   The answer is D.

Radon is a colorless, odorless gas that has been shown to cause lung cancer. It is found in the earth. Testing is a relatively simple and inexpensive process. The Environmental Protection Agency (EPA) has determined that no action is required if the level of radon detected is less than 4 pCi/L (picocuries per liter). However, because this site shows an elevated radon reading, it should be monitored with periodic testing. Should an addition be constructed, steps should be taken to reduce radon levels by providing proper ventilation of spaces in direct contact with the earth.

Appropriate remedial actions for concentrations over 4 pCi/L include sealing any cracks in the foundation walls or floor slab and ventilating or depressurizing the basement or crawlspace area. The EPA recommends that new residences be built with radon-resistant techniques, which are explained in detail on their website, www.epa.gov.

78. The answer is B.

The secretary of the interior's *Standards for the Treatment of Historic Properties* are guidelines established for owners and architects contemplating projects at sites deemed to have historic value. They can be used for any project, but are only required to be followed when federal funding is sought for the project or if the owner plans to apply for Federal Historic Preservation Tax Incentives. Rehabilitation is the most lenient of the four approaches, and the one that best allows for new construction (additions or renovations) and adaptive reuse.

An electronic version of the *Standards* may be downloaded from the National Park Service website at www.cr.nps.gov. A current link to the document can be found at **www.ppi2pass.com/AREresources.**

79. The answer is B.

Batter boards are temporary supports erected to hold wires or strings that indicate the excavation line for a building site. The corners of the building or limits of excavation are marked at the intersection of the lines using a plumb bob. Batter boards are preferred to corner stakes or pins (which are placed at the corners of the structure) because they are set back from the excavation line and will not be disturbed during construction operations.

Grade stakes are used to indicate how much cut or fill is required at a specific location to reach finish grade. They are set by a survey crew and reset periodically as excavation is taking place to monitor progress.

A *transit* is a surveying tool used to determine the elevations of points on a site. It is typically mounted on a tripod for stability. Transits can be as sophisticated as a laser level with a sight that "shoots" elevations using a prism, or as simple as a handheld scope.

80. The answer is A.

The Eiffel Tower, designed by Gustav Eiffel and built for the 1889 World's Fair in Paris, is constructed of wrought iron. In period accounts, the construction material is often referred to as "puddled" iron.

81. The answer is A.

For a commercial toilet room, it is best to use vitreous tile to withstand moisture and harsh chemical cleaners. *Vitrification* is a process of applying heat to a tile to fuse the material and make it denser. Denser tile permits less water to be absorbed. Specifying the level of vitrification is a way of classifying tile based upon its moisture absorption rate.

nonvitreous	7% to 15% absorption
semivitreous	3% to 7% absorption
vitreous	0.05% to 3% absorption
impervious	almost no absorption (less than 0.05%)

A wealth of information about tile's properties and recommended installation details can be found in the *Tile Council of America Handbook for Ceramic Tile Installation*, which is available for purchase from the Tile Council of North America's website, www.tileusa.com, and can be found in most firms' libraries or obtained from a ceramic tile manufacturer's architectural representative.

82. The answer is C.

Heavy crown molds are often made up of a number of different millwork profiles. Millwork is decorative trim produced in a shop, or mill, and delivered to the job site. (*Finish carpentry* is detailed carpentry completed on site, including installation of the millwork.) An advantage to this type of construction is that it visually minimizes any irregularities between the wall and ceiling surfaces, and any gaps can be sealed with caulk and painted. It also offers the architect the opportunity to design a unique profile using standard components and to control the size and proportions of the trim.

Crown molding, option A, forms a link between that wall and the ceiling when installed on an angle and often is made up of a combination of straight cuts and curves. A *cove molding,* option B, features a smooth concave curve. An *architrave,* option C, is a flat piece that is applied directly to the wall.

Picture mold, option D, is mounted a short distance below the built-up crown molding. Its curved top and the space between the picture mold and the bottom of the rest of the crown allows small hooks to be placed over it so that artwork can be suspended from the wall without putting holes into the wall's surface. The entire assembly, picture mold included, is often painted the same color to look like one entity.

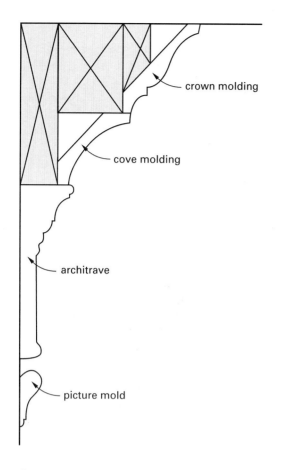

crown molding

cove molding

architrave

picture mold

83.   The answer is C.

The most common grade of plywood used for roof sheathing is C-D Exterior, sometimes referred to as CDX. The Engineered Wood Association classifies plywood veneers into six grades, as follows.

N	natural finish, free of defects
A	smooth and paintable
B	solid-surface veneer
C plugged	splits limited to $^1/_8$ in (3) width and knot/borer holes limited to $^1/_4$ in (6) by $^1/_2$ in (12)
C	knotholes permitted to 1 in (25). Limited splits permitted. Minimum grade for exterior plywood.
D	knots/knotholes to 3 in (76) permitted. Limited splits permitted.

The first letter indicates the classification of the face ply (the highest-grade side) of the plywood. (If both sides have the same classification, they are both referred to as faces.) The second letter indicates the classification of the back ply (the lower-grade side) of the material. If the plywood is marked exterior, it contains plies bonded with exterior glue.

More information about plywood, including the *Panel Handbook and Grade Glossary*, can be downloaded in electronic format from The Engineered Wood Association's website, www.apawood.org. (Registration is required.)

84.   The answer is D.

U bead, also sometimes called *J bead* or *J metal*, is the only edge treatment listed that does not require finishing with joint compound. It is less expensive to install than the others because it does not require finishing, but the edge treatment is noticeably visible.

The other types of edge treatments are all indented a bit on the face side so that joint compound can be used to fill the gap and the treatment is not noticeable on the finished wall. *LC bead* is the basic edge treatment that requires a layer of compound be applied to conceal the metal. *L bead* does not have a back flange and can be used when the gypsum board is already installed or for repairs to the edge bead. *LK bead* is designed for use with a kerfed jamb.

85.   The answer is B.

A *gearless traction* elevator would be an appropriate choice for the office building. Gearless traction elevators can travel at the highest speeds of the types listed, and to accommodate the rush of people entering and exiting the building in the morning, at lunch time, and in the evening, the quick cycles would be a necessity.

Gearless traction and geared traction are two different types of electric elevators. Both operate on DC current. The *geared traction* elevator travels at slower speeds but offers many options for adjusting the speed to suit the building conditions.

Hydraulic elevators are lifted by a ram, which must be sunk into the ground the same distance as the height of the elevator's path of travel. Therefore, they are used only in low-rise buildings (generally less than six stories). They travel much more slowly than electric elevators and are better used for freight or for low-occupancy passenger elevators where speed is not an issue.

PRACTICE EXAM: VIGNETTE SOLUTIONS

ACCESSIBILITY/RAMP: PASSING SOLUTION

This vignette requires the candidate to understand basic code requirements for ramp and stair layout. This includes maintaining maximum ramp slopes, proper design of handrails, and correct stair design. It also tests application of knowledge about egress doors and accessible maneuvering clearances at doors and ramps.

Solving Approach

Step 1 Locate the required new wall and doors. Because the existing doors were double, they should be duplicated on the assumption that this was the required exit width. Swing the doors in the direction of travel and maintain maneuvering clearances on both the pull and push sides of the doors. In the vestibule, maintain at least 48 in (1220) between the edge of the existing door when open and the new wall.

Step 2 Lay out the ramps, maintaining a maximum 1:12 slope. In this case, because the level change is 30 in (760) there must be at least 30 ft (9145) of horizontal ramp length. Although the ramps can be as narrow as 44 in, making them 60 in (1525) wide makes it easier to provide correct landing sizes.

Step 3 At each landing, provide a 60 in (1525) minimum landing size. Because the ramp handrail must extend 12 in (305) beyond the top of the ramp, the landing has been made 72 in (1830) long.

Step 4 Show all required handrails on both sides of the ramp and stair. Extend the handrails 12 in (305) beyond the top and bottom of the ramp and stair unless it is continuous.

Step 5 Show a guard at the level change and at each landing as required.

Step 6 Try to place the lower level of the ramp near the lower level of the stair. Make sure the remaining space is accessible.

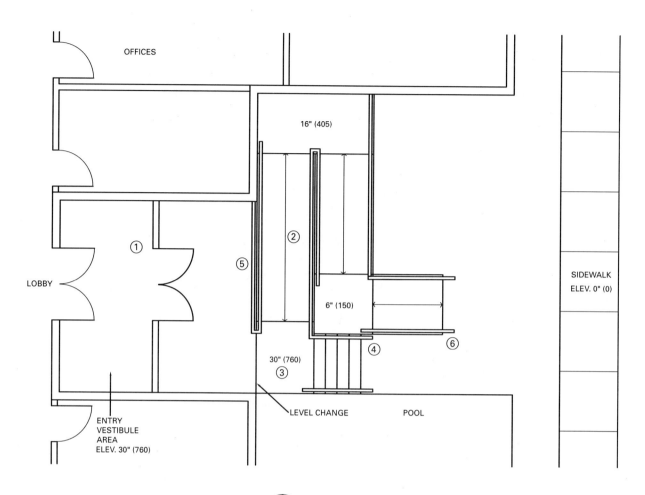

OFFICES

16" (405)

②

LOBBY

⑤

⑥

6" (150)

④

30" (760)
③

LEVEL CHANGE   POOL

ENTRY
VESTIBULE
AREA
ELEV. 30" (760)

SIDEWALK
ELEV. 0" (0)

①

Scale: 1/8" = 1'-0"
(1:100 metric)   ACCESSIBILITY/RAMP:
PASSING SOLUTION

ACCESSIBILITY/RAMP: FAILING SOLUTION

Pitfalls

Note 1 There is not enough space between the end of the existing door and the new wall. A distance of at least 48 in (1220) is required.

Note 2 The guard for the upper level has been omitted.

Note 3 There is no extension on the upper ramp handrail.

Note 4 There is no extension on the lower ramp handrail.

Note 5 Because this stair is 6 ft (1830) wide, there must be an intermediate handrail.

Note 6 The first portion of the ramp is less than 10 ft (3050) long, resulting in a slope greater than 1:12.

Note 7 The ramp handrail extensions project into the normal approach space to the stair. This is undesirable, though not a critical error.

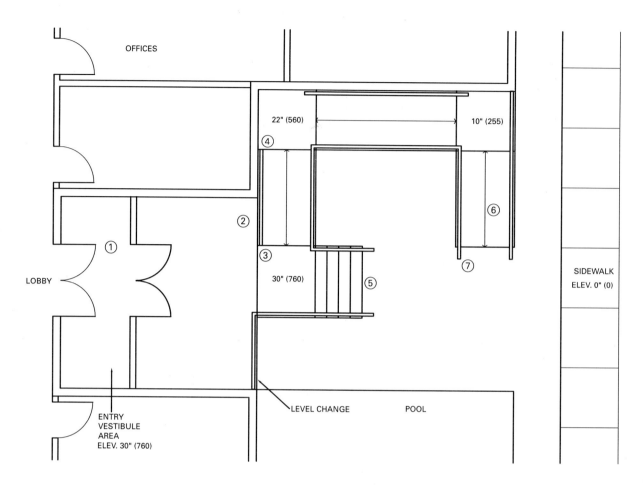

OFFICES

22" (560)   10" (255)

④

②

①

LOBBY

③

30" (760)

⑤

⑥

⑦

SIDEWALK
ELEV. 0" (0)

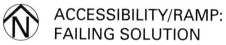

LEVEL CHANGE   POOL

ENTRY
VESTIBULE
AREA
ELEV. 30" (760)

Scale: 1/8" = 1'-0"
(1:100 metric)

Ⓝ

ACCESSIBILITY/RAMP:
FAILING SOLUTION

ROOF PLAN: PASSING SOLUTION

This vignette tests the candidate's understanding of roof slope and accommodation of various elements for the roof plan of a building. The vignette presents a background floor plan with the edges of two roofs shown, one low and one high, and the candidate must complete a roof plan with roof slopes, spot elevations, and symbols for various roof elements that are required by the program.

Solving Approach

Step 1 Decide on the basic configuration of the roof slopes. If possible, use a simple gable configuration for both the lower and upper roofs. Keep in mind that it is best if the ridge of the lower roof along the clerestory is parallel with the lower edge of the upper roof. With a simple configuration, it is less likely that mistakes will be made figuring the elevations and slopes, especially when time is short.

Step 2 Draw the clerestory location as required by the program.

Step 3 Starting with the lowest portion of the lower roof, set the elevation of the roof, adding the ceiling height given in the program to the total thickness of the roof structure.

Step 4 Set the slope of the lower roof, using a slope at the low range of the allowable slopes.

Step 5 Calculate the elevation at the highest point of the lower roof using the slope determined in Step 3.

Step 6 Determine the low point of the upper roof by adding the clerestory height requirement to the roof structure thickness.

Step 7 Set the slope of the upper roof, staying within the allowable range given in the program.

Step 8 If the configuration of the roof requires it, add crickets where a roof slope intersects a roof penetration.

Step 9 Add flashing wherever the roof intersects a wall or other vertical surface.

Step 10 Add gutters and downspouts at the low portions of all roofs.

Step 11 Set the location of the HVAC condenser unit, maintaining the minimum distance from roof edges and making sure it is not in front of the clerestory.

Step 12 Add stack vents wherever plumbing requires it. Show exhaust fans in the toilet rooms. Add skylights to any interior room that requires them.

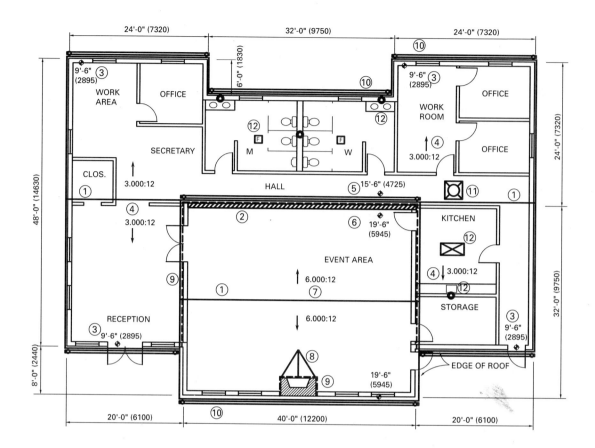

Scale: 1/16" = 1'-0"
(1:200 metric)

ROOF PLAN:
PASSING SOLUTION

ROOF PLAN: FAILING SOLUTION

Pitfalls

Note 1 There is insufficient clearance between the lower roof and the lower portions of the upper roof to accommodate the roof structure and the clerestory window.

Note 2 If a 4.000:12 roof slope is used as indicated, the high edges of the east and west roofs will not match up with the high edge of the north roof.

Note 3 Gutters are missing along a short portion of the upper roof.

Note 4 A downspout is missing. Although this is not a specific requirement and would not cause the solution to fail, a downspout should be placed at each end of a gutter.

Note 5 A vent stack is missing for the kitchen sink.

Note 6 There is no flashing at the chimney/roof intersection.

Note 7 The HVAC condensing unit is too close to the edge of the roof.

Note 8 A skylight is required in the kitchen.

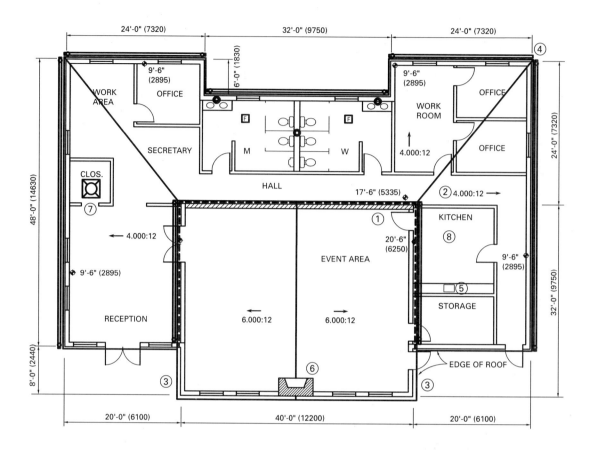

Scale: 1/16" = 1'-0"
(1:200 metric)

ROOF PLAN:
FAILING SOLUTION

STAIR DESIGN: PASSING SOLUTION

This vignette tests the candidate's understanding of the three-dimensional nature of stair design and the basic functional and code issues involved. The vignette presents two background floor plans, a building section, a program, and code requirements; the candidate must complete a floor plan with a stair system.

Solving Approach

Step 1 Determine the width of the stairs from both the second level and the lower level. In this case, the stair from the second level requires a width greater than the 44 in (1120) minimum (160 occupants × 0.3 in/occupant = 48 in (1220)). The stairway from the lower level requires a 60 in (1525) wide stair (200 occupants × 0.3 in/occupant = 60 in (1525)).

Step 2 Determine the number of risers required. First determine the number of risers required from the second level to the lower level. In this case, the difference between 15 ft 10 in (4825) and 3 ft 0 in (915) can be evenly divided by 7 in (178) risers for a total of 22 required risers.

Step 3 Determine the number of refuge spaces required at each level. Because there are two exits from the second level required for a total occupant load of 320, only 160 people are served by this exit; therefore, only one refuge space is required. For the lower level, two refuge spaces are required. Using a sketch rectangle is a good way to make sure sufficient space is available.

Step 4 Lay out the stair configuration so that the stair from the second level returns to the area near the door to the lower level. Make the return landing such that there will be sufficient headroom for the travel path from the mechanical room door to the exit door at grade level.

Step 5 Make sure that the landings are of sufficient size to allow for maneuvering clearances at the side of the door and that the swing of the door when opening does not decrease the width of the landing by more than one half.

Step 6 Set the elevation of all landings and the top and bottom of each stair flight.

Step 7 Draw in handrails and guards for the stairs and landings. Make sure that if the stair handrails are not continuous, they extend 12 in (305) beyond the bottom and top risers.

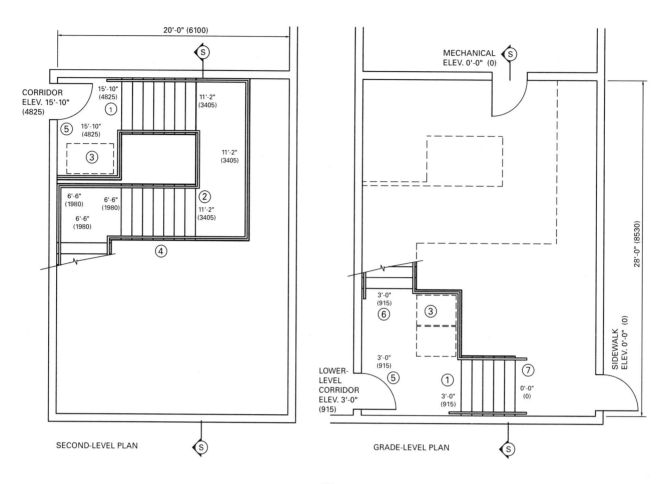

SECOND-LEVEL PLAN

GRADE-LEVEL PLAN

Scale: 1/8" = 1'-0"
(1:100 metric)

STAIR DESIGN:
PASSING SOLUTION

STAIR DESIGN: FAILING SOLUTION

Pitfalls

Note 1 Two refuge spaces are provided when only one is required.

Note 2 Although the landing of the second level is of sufficient size, it is too large.

Note 3 Only one refuge space is provided when two are required.

Note 4 The stair leading from the lower level to the grade level is too narrow.

Note 5 The handrails for the stairs at the grade level do not extend the required 12 in (305).

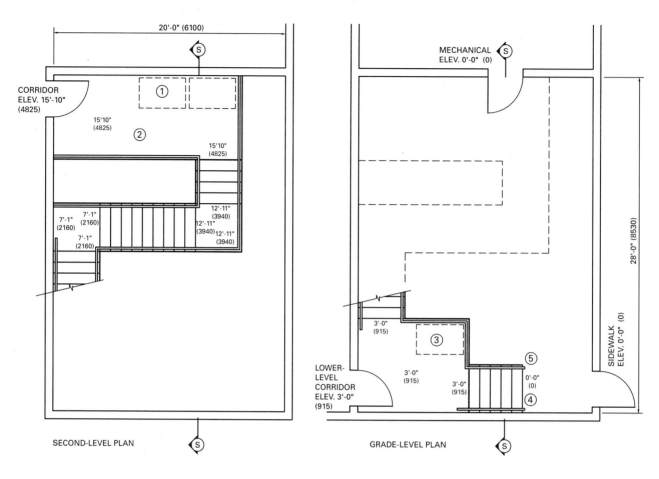

20'-0" (6100)

CORRIDOR
ELEV. 15'-10"
(4825)

①

15'10"
(4825)   ②

15'10"
(4825)

12'-11"
(3940)
12'-11"
(3940) 12'-11"
(3940)

7'-1"
(2160)   7'-1"
(2160)

7'-1"
(2160)

7'-1"
(2160)

SECOND-LEVEL PLAN

MECHANICAL
ELEV. 0'-0" (0)

28'-0" (8530)

SIDEWALK
ELEV. 0'-0" (0)

3'-0"
(915)

③

⑤

LOWER-
LEVEL
CORRIDOR
ELEV. 3'-0"
(915)

3'-0"
(915)

3'-0"
(915)

0'-0"
(0)

④

GRADE-LEVEL PLAN

Scale: 1/8" = 1'-0"
(1:100 metric)

**STAIR DESIGN:
FAILING SOLUTION**